The Joy of Flint

An Introduction to Stone Tools and
Guide to the Museum of Antiquities Collection

**Museum of Antiquities
University of Newcastle-upon-Tyne**

© Museum of Antiquities, Newcastle-upon-Tyne

ISBN 0 7017 0165 X
First printed 2004

Published by: Museum of Antiquities, University of Newcastle upon Tyne
Designed by: www.thedesigndesk.co.uk
Illustrations: Ben Johnson
Photography: © Peter Forrester

Front cover: John Lord photographed during filming of
BBC television's 'Meet the Ancestors' programme.

Back cover: A view of Milfield Basin looking towards Kimmerston.

Contents

DATE Calendar years BC	ARCHAEO-LOGICAL PERIOD	CULTURAL TERMS	GEO-LOGICAL PERIOD	HOMINIDS	LITHIC TRADITIONS	EXAMPLES
1500	Early Bronze Age				Wide variety of exotic tools. e.g. sickles and copies of metal objects such as daggers. Proliferation of poor quality flake tools for everyday use.	
2500	Later Neolithic				Invasive retouch Flake tools and less reliance on blade technology Grinding and polishing	
3200	Early Neolithic				Blade based industries Invasive retouch Grinding and polishing Platform cores Use of microliths abandoned Bifacial retouch common	
4000	Later Mesolithic	Tardenoisian, Sauveterrian, *and others.*	∧		Narrow blade microliths Geometric microliths Abrupt retouch, usually unifacial only Platform cores	
8000	Early Mesolithic	Maglemosian, Azilian, *and others.*	Flandrian/Holocene		Broad blade microliths Burins Abrupt retouch Blade tools Platform cores	
10000	Late Upper Palaeolithic	Creswellian, Hamburgian, Magdalenian, *and others.*	Loch Lomond Stadial		Blade technology Creswellian points Cheddar points Platform cores	
15000	Upper Palaeolithic	Magdalenian, Solutrean, Gravettian, Aurignacian, Châtelperronian, *and others.*	∧	Modern *Homo Sapiens*	Blade technology Long blade tools including abrupt and invasive retouch. Unifacial and bifacial blade tools Laurel leaf points Shouldered points Burins	
40000	Middle Palaeolithic	Mousterian	Devensian	Early *Homo Sapiens* (Neanderthals)	Flat based (bout coupé) hand axes Development of Levallois tradition Flake tools	
		Levallois	Ipswichian 120-110K			
200000			Wolstonian		Hand axes and range of biface tools Scrapers	
	Lower Palaeolithic	Acheulian	Hoxnian 250-350K	*Homo erectus* (hominid)		
			Anglian	**Earliest known Palaeolithic occupation of Britain**		
500000		Clactonian	Cromerian 350-500K			
2000000		Oldowan		*Homo habilis* (hominid)	Core tools Pebble tools	

1 - Chronological summary of stone tool traditions.

List of Illustrations

Acknowledgements

This book sprang from conversations between Lindsay Allason-Jones (Director of Archaeological Museums, University of Newcastle) and the author over coffee among the finds-boxes, artefacts, Roman replica shields and the like in the Museum of Antiquities' office. It was recognised that there was a need for both a guide to the impressive lithic artefact collections of the Museum on the one hand and an introductory text for the study of stone tools on the other. Indeed, the need for an up-to-date text dealing with stone tools became even more compelling after we had started teaching a new undergraduate module in artefact studies at the University of Newcastle. As the over-reliance on archaeological theory in undergraduate archaeological teaching is reigned in and we return, albeit more critically aware, to artefact studies, it is hoped that texts such as this will go some way to reintroducing budding archaeologists to the nuts and bolts of archaeology: namely artefacts and structures. For making this idea possible and commenting on the text particular thanks are owed to Lindsay who has provided support and assistance throughout. The Society of Antiquaries of Newcastle upon Tyne deserve special thanks for providing the resources to write and publish this book. I would also like to record my gratitude to Frances Healy, Kristian Pedersen, Alan Saville, David Schofield and Rob Young for reading and commenting on the text and to Ben Johnson for producing the illustrations and Peter Forrester for his excellent photographs and book layout. I would also like to acknowledge the many publications from which a number of the illustrations have been redrawn and adapted, and in particular the book by Whittaker (1994). Alan Saville has kindly allowed me to reproduce Figure 13 and likewise Peter Topping has allowed me to reproduce Figures 12 and 15. I am also grateful to Jon Humble who drew my attention to the biblical reference concerning flint knives and the ritual of circumcision (page 50).

Finally, I would like to thank all the people who took part in my Stone Age fieldwalking project in the Milfield Basin over the last few years and for helping to sample across over 15 million square metres of ploughsoil. It is to them that I dedicate this book.

The Museum of Antiquities is grateful to the Society of Antiquaries of Newcastle-upon-Tyne, the Roland Cookson Charitable Trust and Tarmac plc for their financial assistance in the publication of this book.

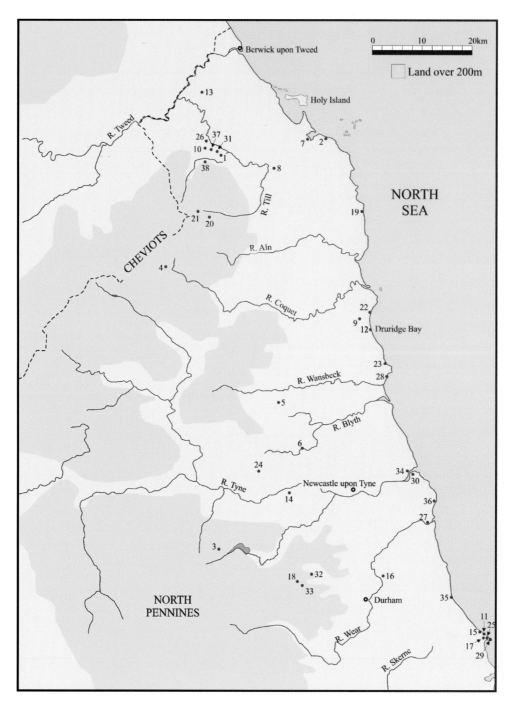

1 Akeld Steads, 2 Bamburgh, 3 Birkside Fell, 4 Black Stitchell Rigg, 5 Bolam Lake,
6 Braid Hill, 7 Budle Bay, 8 Chatton Park Hill, 9 Chevington, 10 Coupland,
11 Crimdon Dene, 12 Druridge Bay, 13 Duddo Stone Circle, 14 Eltringham Farm,
15 Filpoke Beacon, 16 Finchale Nab, 17 Hart, 18 Horsley Burn, 19 Howick, 20 Ingram Hill, 21
Linhope Burn, 22 Low Hauxley, 23 Lyne Hill, 24 Matfen Standing Stone,
25 Middle Warren, 26 Milfield, 27 Monkwearmouth, 28 Newbiggin-by-the-Sea,
29 Seaton Carew, 30 South Shields, 31 Thirlings, 32 Tunstall Reservoir, 33 Unthank, 34 Wallsend,
35 Warren House Gill, 36 Whitburn, 37 Woodbridge Farm, 38 Yeavering

2 - Map of north-east England showing the location of key Stone Age sites.

Introduction

The aims of this book are to present the reader with an introduction to the study of stone tools as practiced in Britain and to provide a guide to the lithic collections held by the Museum of Antiquities of the University and Society of Antiquaries of Newcastle upon Tyne. It is by no means definitive nor in-depth but rather an attempt to provide an entry into the world of lithic studies. The intention throughout has been to present an accessible introduction to stone tools aimed at the newcomer to the subject, particularly the undergraduate student and interested reader. The bibliography is intended to be extensive, with direction for further reading indicated throughout the text. By using the bibliography and the references contained in those sources the reader will be able to gain access to a wide range of more specialist publications. As publications on lithic artefacts tend to be dominated by accounts based on southern collections this text will, in contrast, offer a northern perspective as it is based on the lithic artefact collections of a northern regional Museum.

The book is divided into two sections. The first part contains the general introduction to stone tools followed by the further information section. The second half contains the gazetteer for the Museum's lithic collections. The gazetteer does not include references to the large stone axe head collection held by the Museum of Antiquities (over 175) although it does include the flint axes. Inclusion of the stone axe corpus was considered beyond the scope of this publication, deserving a full publication in its own right. I have also included a short glossary to help define specialist terms and to avoid definitions that would otherwise break up the main body of the text and make referencing somewhat arduous.

For much of the Ice Age, northern Britain was either under ice or experiencing erosive periglacial conditions at the ice margins with the result that this area has little surviving evidence of Palaeolithic settlement. Therefore, more space is given to discussion of later periods for which there is more surviving material in the north-east.

Stone tool types show considerable variation through time and distinctive types are associated with different archaeological periods. Although much simplified, Figure 1 attempts to summarise the changes in lithic technology through time. It may be useful for the reader to refer to this when consulting the period specific chapters. Figure 2 shows the location of the key Stone Age sites in the north-east of England mentioned in the text.

Because the study of stone tools continually reveals unexpected information, research needs to continue into museum collections as well as newly discovered material. With this in mind, assemblages in the Museum of Antiquities' collection which would repay further attention have been highlighted in the hope that students and academics will take up the challenge.

3 - Flint nodules from primary chalk deposits

4 - Chert from north-east England

5 - Quartz from north-east England

6 - Agate from north-east England

1. Lithic Raw Materials

For most of human history people have relied on stone as one of the principal raw materials for making tools. Stone is a highly durable, naturally occurring material that can produce sharp, blunted or serrated edges by a simple blow using another stone or an antler hammer. Furthermore, different stones have different properties that allow them to be utilised for a wide variety of purposes. Tools made from various types of stone are found throughout Britain (in this book the term "stone" is used interchangeably with the term "rock").

Rock suitable for making chipped stone tools is usually of fine-grained, uniform structure and smooth texture. In addition it needs to be hard and brittle and, ideally, to fracture conchoidally (Andrefsky 1998). A conchoidal fracture is the detachment of a stone flake in a shell-like fashion across a uniform plane. These properties allow stone to be chipped in a controlled way with predictable results. They allow very sharp edges and points to be produced as well as long thin blades that can be further modified into specific tool forms. This means that the number of rocks that can be used effectively for stone tool production is limited, compared to the actual number of rock types that exist in these islands. Our prehistoric forebears must have been discerning rock-hunters, well aware of rock characteristics and, perhaps, able to predict the location of likely sources.

Types

Flint

Flint is really a type of silica (see also below), though it is discussed separately here as it is the dominant type of stone tool raw material used in the British Isles during the Stone Age. Its shiny lustre, varied colours, ease of flaking and aesthetically pleasing look and feel probably added to the special regard in which this rock was held by our ancestors, particularly as it also provided a rapid spark-making device for making fire. How flint is formed remains an area of debate within geology and this uncertainty adds to the mystique surrounding the origins and perceptions of this material. It is, however, generally thought to form in a deep-sea environment from silica-secreting organisms, particularly diatoms (algae with silicified skeletons), which undergo a process of silica transformation (see Andrefsky 1998, 52-3 or Williams and Crerar 1985 for fuller description).

Flint is found in the British Isles in chalk deposits dating from the Upper Cretaceous period (around 95-65 million years ago). It also occurs in secondary drift deposits (such as boulder clay or gravels) where it was deposited by ice sheets or their meltwaters after the erosion and transportation of primary flint bearing deposits during the various glaciations. Flint comes in all shapes and sizes from tiny pebbles and fist-sized nodules, to laterally bedded horizons of large nodules in sedimentary chalk sequences. It can be white, red, orange, purple, yellow, brown, ginger or black although it most commonly occurs as shades of grey and sometimes as a mixture of these colours. Flint can also be speckled and sometimes contains impurities that may or may not affect the fracturing properties of the piece. As with the other types of silicious material, flint can develop a patina, or altered surface texture/colour, as a result of chemical processes over time. It is thought that this involves the refilling of emptied pores within the flint's structure with silica derived from soil water (Shepherd 1972), though the whole question of patina development, the effects of different environmental settings, and the rate at which patination occurs over time on silica rock types, are topics greatly in need of further research (Schmalz 1960).

Varieties of Silica

Flint (Fig. 3), chert (Fig. 4), quartz (Fig. 5), agate (Fig. 6), chalcedony, bloodstone, jasper and onyx (among others), are all forms of silica (SiO2) and are chemically identical, apart from minor traces of other elements. They are composed of the elements silicon and oxygen and are, therefore, known as silica or silica dioxide. These types of rock can occur in an igneous or sedimentary context. The most common types of silica used for stone tool production are those with an amorphous, non-crystalline structure such as those mentioned above. These types of silica all possess conchoidal fracturing properties, although the various types usually have a

7 - Quartz outcropping in granite (Glencoe, Scotland)

distinctive appearance and colour. Flint and chert form as nodules in layers in chalk and limestone while the other varieties of silica form as minerals within the cavities and fissures of parent rocks (Fig. 7) such as the mineral veins or gas cavities in igneous rocks. The 'topstone' and 'wallstone' flint seams identified at Grime's Graves, Norfolk, provide a good example of flint nodule layers in chalk deposits while the 'floorstone' at the same site is found as intermittent blocks known as semi-tabular deposits.

Flint is generally located in the south and east of Britain, associated with chalk deposits, while chert can be found with the hard limestone formations that occur in the Midlands, Wales, and the North, particularly in the Pennines (Fig. 8). However, no less important sources of stone tool material are the flints and associated silica rocks that occur in derived geological contexts. Derived deposits are composed of material that has been eroded from primary deposits and then transported (usually by glacial or fluvial action) to a new location where they are redeposited. Typical geological situations where raw materials occur as derived deposits include river gravels, boulder clay and other tills, such as clay-with-flints, together with beach deposits (Fig. 8). Such sources are particularly significant in regions of Britain distant from the primary flint sources. In the case of north-east England, for example, the nearest source of primary flint is the chalk Wolds of east Yorkshire while derived sources of flint can be found in the boulder clays which mantle the coastal margins of north-east Yorkshire (a light grey speckled flint), County Durham (a grey-orange and ginger flint), and Northumberland (light grey, grey-orange and red-brown flint). However, flint can also be found in pebble form on the beaches of north-east England where it is often orange or grey in colour, though it often has a thick cortex of a different colour (Fig. 9).

Primary flint, often referred to as 'nodular flint', is usually dark grey or black in colour (Fig. 3). It has a soft white chalky cortex (outer crust) and is generally a very high quality material for stone tool production. Flint from derived deposits is usually, though not always, of inferior quality, a good example of an exception being the light grey, speckled, boulder clay flint of north-east Yorkshire. Although derived flint usually occurs in small nodules this does not mean that these sources were any less important to the people who used them. Rather, analysis of the flintwork from north-east England suggests people employed specific flaking strategies to make the best use of the materials at their disposal. This included keeping lithic tools small, recycling old tools into new ones once their initial use had ended and simply becoming adept at the more difficult task of making tools from less easily flaked materials. Derived flint is sometimes referred to as 'beach pebble flint' or 'glacial flint' or 'boulder clay flint' depending on its origin. The cortex of beach pebble flint is characterised by a thick hard coat that has been smoothed and rounded by sea action. They can be difficult to distinguish from other stone pebbles, although those found on the north-east coast often have an orange-brown cortex. Boulder clay flint usually has a thin cortex and an abraded surface, usually resembling the colour of the flint, although sometimes it may retain thin or patchy areas of white chalky cortex surviving from its original primary context.

8 - Location of major chipped stone sources.

9 - Beach flint from north-east England

Chert typically forms in hard limestone deposits (non-chalk) either as individual nodules or in layers. Agates can also form in limestone, although they are more common in volcanic rocks such as granite or andesite. Banding, which is particularly common in agates, occurs as a result of incremental silica formation within a rock cavity, with each band representing a separate phase of silica formation.

Agates, quartz and volcanic glass are most frequently located alongside the volcanic rocks that are generally located in the north and west of Britain and in the Greensands of the south-west. Derived deposits can also be found throughout the north-east and include the characteristic banded agates found in the gravel terraces of the Milfield Plain together with quartz, chert and occasionally volcanic glass, while cherts also occur in quantities in the outwash gravels from the Carboniferous Limestone regions of the Pennines and Magnesian Limestone of County Durham.

Quartz is the term used to refer to the varieties of silica that form in a regular crystalline structure and typically occurs in granites and sandstone (Fig. 7). Although quartz is a major constituent of materials such as sandstone, it is the quartz that occurs in discrete lumps as rock crystals or crystalline aggregates that was used for chipping into stone tools. These rock crystals can fracture conchoidally, or almost conchoidally, and in their purest form can appear as a translucent material not dissimilar to glass. Quartz can produce sharp edges when flaked and can be made into scraper-type tools and points. Quartz crystals used for making stone tools can be found in glacial deposits as well as in river gravel and beach deposits. These crystals are used for making stone tools, particularly in areas where good quality raw materials, such as flint, are scarce - as in north Northumberland and Scotland (see for example, Saville and Ballin 2000). Quartz occurs frequently in drift deposits throughout the north-east although areas which consistently produce quartz artefacts include the Tyne Valley and the areas in and around the Milfield Basin.

Limestone
Limestone is a sedimentary rock made from fossilized sea creatures whose main chemical constituents are calcium carbonate ($CaCO_3$). Although it does not fracture conchoidally, and is thus more difficult to flake, it can produce sharp edges and was, therefore, occasionally used to make stone tools.

Volcanic and Other Igneous Rocks
Volcanic rocks which can be used to make chipped stone tools include andesite, basalt and rhyolite, particularly when they occur as fine-grained tuffs. The various stone types used to make ground and polished stone axe heads in the British Isles have been divided into distinct 'groups' by petrologists based on the source of the stone (Clough and Cummins 1979; 1988). In northern England this includes the quartz dolerite rock of the Great Whin Sill, a basaltic formation of intrusive igneous rock that formed

10 - Examples of a rock pounder, a roughout and a finished stone axe made from Langdale tuff, Cumbria

during the Carboniferous period. The Whin Sill extends from the Vale of Eden in the west and under much of Durham and Northumberland, to the Farne Islands in the east. It outcrops in various places, notably in Upper Teesdale, along the central sector of Hadrian's Wall and on the Northumberland coast. Whinstone is known to have been used for the production of ground and polished stone axe heads during the Neolithic period and the shaft-hole implements of the Early Bronze Age. These are referred to as Group XVIII rocks (see Evens *et al* 1962; Clough and Cummins 1979; 1988, 80). An area in Upper Teesdale has been suggested as a likely source by archaeologists (Keen and Radley 1971, 25-7), although Burgess (1984, 136) and Cummins and Harding (1988, 80) have reported the discovery of the first recognised working floor at Cullernose Point on the Northumberland coast. Cummins and Harding contest whether prehistoric people could have chipped the dolerite whereas others argue that it was pecked rather than flaked. The recent finds of dolerite stone axe roughouts and associated chips at Howick suggest the material was chipped and that the outcrop at Howick Scar was also used as a quarry. The Whinstone can also be collected as rolled cobbles on the beach and the opportunistic use of pieces from river beds and gravel deposits may have also been important.

The volcanic tuff of the Lake District is particularly significant as it can be easily flaked due to its fine texture. This rock appears to have been the most prolific source of material used for stone axes in Britain. Although most of these Group VI axe heads are ground and polished in their finished form, they were initially roughed into shape by flaking (Fig. 10). See the publication by Bradley and Edmonds (1993) for a recent discussion of the 'axe trade' in relation to the Lake District sources.

Andesite occurs in north and western Britain and outcrops in the Cheviot Hills of Northumberland as well as in the volcanic hills of western Britain, Scotland and Ireland. It is a type of pyroclastic volcanic lava that can be chipped or ground and polished into tools (Fig. 11). Andesite stone axe head roughouts were initially chipped into shape at the Rathlin Island (Ireland) source and at Tievebulliagh (Antrim, Ireland) and possibly at the as yet unidentified andesite axe source in the Upper Breamish Valley/Threestoneburn area of the Cheviot Hills (Waddington and Schofield 1999).

Volcanic glass was also used to make stone tools. Fast-cooling igneous rocks, such as obsidian, cool with such speed that crystals do not have time to grow. This produces a naturally formed glass which, because of its homogeneous nature, is an ideal material for making stone tools (Andrefsky 1998, 46). It usually occurs as a shiny black material although it can be greenish and have red or green patches. There are no known obsidian sources in the British Isles though sources have been found in Italy, Poland and Turkey. Other types of volcanic glass are found in the British Isles and include the black to green, though less shiny, pitchstone, which has its main sources on the island of Arran (Affleck *et al* 1988) though it does occur elsewhere, such as Blindburn near Alwinton, Northumberland. Pitchstone is virtually identical to obsidian mineralogically although it has a slight microcrystalline structure that means that its conchoidal fracturing properties are not quite as true as obsidian. Although pitchstone is chemically identical to granite, the rapid cooling of pitchstone means that it does not share the large crystalline structure characteristic of granites.

Acquisition
Both primary stone tool material and derived stone tool material can be acquired by surface collection or open-cast quarrying. For example, primary nodular flint can be collected from exposed seams in chalk cliff

11 - Stone axes made from north-eastern rock: Cheviot andesite from the Milfield Basin and Fellsandstone from Berwick

12 - View of the 'lunar' ground surface in the central section of the Grimes Graves mines complex, Norfolk (Photo: © Pete Topping)

faces, from the ground surface where nodules are exposed, or from drift mining along a seam that outcrops on a slope. Derived material can also be acquired by the same methods as well as by collection from exposed stream banks, gravel deposits and glacial drift and by collection from the beach where flint is washed in by the tide. Volcanic glass and igneous rock can be won by surface collection, particularly from screes, as well as from open-cast quarrying where igneous formations outcrop above ground.

Such methods of extraction characterised all lithic raw material acquisition during the Palaeolithic and Mesolithic periods. However, with the onset of the Neolithic a new method for acquiring large quantities of raw material was adopted: the flint mine. This intensification of nodular flint exploitation, and its use across the whole of the British Isles, suggests that the phenomenon was directly linked to the emergence of effective and far-reaching exchange networks during the Neolithic, marking a departure from locally-based Late Mesolithic socio-economic organisation.

Today prehistoric flint mines are visible on the ground as crater-like lunar landscapes (Fig. 12) produced by the mounds of waste upcast around the shaft heads. All the large flint mine complexes so far recorded in the British Isles are located on the chalk deposits of East Anglia, central southern England and the Sussex coast, with the exception of the important sites on the Buchan Ridge (Fig. 13) in north-east Scotland (Saville 1995). Recently, the RCHME has undertaken a survey that has recorded all known Neolithic flint mines in England (Barber *et al* 1999).

Important archaeological investigations of flint mines have included excavation of shafts and associated galleries within the mining complexes at Grime's Graves (Mercer 1981b; Saville 1981a)

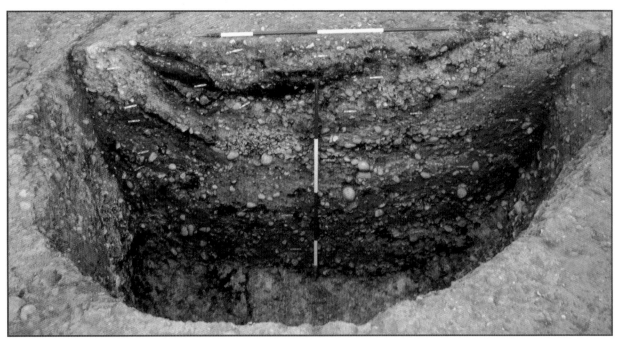

13 - Section through quarry pit 101, one of the Buchan Ridge flint quarries
(Photo: © Alan Saville)

(Fig. 14), Harrow Hill (Curwen and Curwen 1926), Blackpatch (Pull 1932) and Easton Down (Stone 1932), among others. These excavations have shown that the mining procedure could take a variety of forms, including drift mining and open cast mining (Holgate 1991, 11) or by sinking vertical shafts and excavating along radiating galleries following the flint seams (Fig. 15). Such shafts were between 4m and 8m wide and up to 14m deep (Holgate 1991).

The main tools of the Neolithic miner were the red deer antler pick and the mattock (Figs. 15, 16 and 17), although stone and flint-hafted axes were also used. Rubble appears to have been scooped up using ox shoulder blades and possibly wooden shovels, together with antler rakes. Flint was then lifted from the shaft in leather bags or baskets. After a shaft was exhausted it was deliberately backfilled.

It appears that Neolithic people regarded flint mining not just as a functional task but also as a symbolically and ritually ordered activity. At the entrance to one of the galleries in shaft 27 at Cissbury the skeleton of a crouched woman lying on her side was discovered. Three carvings of red deer heads and one of a horned bull were located on one of the gallery walls nearby. It has, however, been suggested that the pile of flint covered by red deer antlers, and associated with a chalk female figurine, a chalk phallus and chalk balls at the entrance to one of the galleries of a Grimes Graves shaft excavated by Armstrong, may have been placed there as a practical joke rather than being a 'votive' offering (Holgate 1991, 30-31; Longworth and Varndell 1996).

Another innovative technique introduced in the Neolithic period was the use of fire-setting. This process involved lighting a fire against a rock face and then cooling the stone quickly by pouring water on it. This

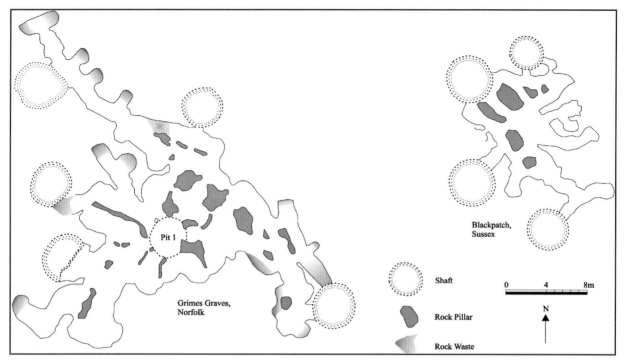

14 - Plans of excavated areas in the Grimes Graves and Blackpatch flint mine complexes
(Redrawn from Holgate 1991 and Barber *et al* 1999)

process forces the rock to crack, making it easier to break off and quarry. Excavations in Langdale, Cumbria, have revealed evidence for the widespread use of this technique (Bradley and Edmonds 1993) to obtain the tuff that was then transformed into stone axe heads for use across the British Isles.

A question that never fails to spring to mind is whether Neolithic pitmen suffered from mining maladies such as chalk

15 - View inside Gallery III, 'Greenwell's Pit' (Grimes Graves), with antler picks abandoned next to the flint layer or 'floorstone' (Photo: © Pete Topping)

dust inhalation, silicosis or arthritis or from accidents such as roof collapse. The recent Brandon flint knappers are known to have suffered from silicosis but they worked long hours, full-time and in crowded conditions. How serious a problem this may have been for what were presumably seasonal Neolithic flint miners remains unknown, although the example of the Neolithic flint miner killed as the result of a roof collapse, still clutching an antler pick, at Spiennes in Belgium (Hubert 1988; 1990), serves as a reminder of the perils of underground working. Could the danger and darkness associated

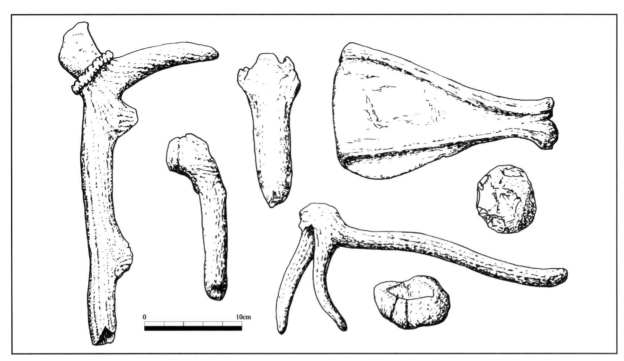

16 - Examples of various flint mining tools (Redrawn from Holgate 1991)

with prehistoric flint mining have prompted the need for observing rituals and placating spirits? It was certainly a concern for later lead miners who, in the Peak District, referred to the spirit of a mine as "T'Owd Mon". On the other hand, flint mining appears to be yet another expression of the Neolithic obsession with the ground, shown by pit and ditch digging, and the placing of ritual deposits in pits, caves and chambered tombs, all of which imply a need to propitiate spirits through ritual within the context of the earth. Furthermore, the ethnographic record has provided evidence for the importance of symbolism, myth and ritual associated with chert extraction in the Americas (e.g. Justice 1989).

A useful list of flint mine sites and museums to visit can be found in the publication by Holgate (1991, 51-53) while a more socially oriented approach to the process of flint mining and stone quarrying is convincingly articulated by Edmonds (1995, 59-66). The most recent and valuable survey of Neolithic flint mines in England is that by Barber *et al.* (1999).

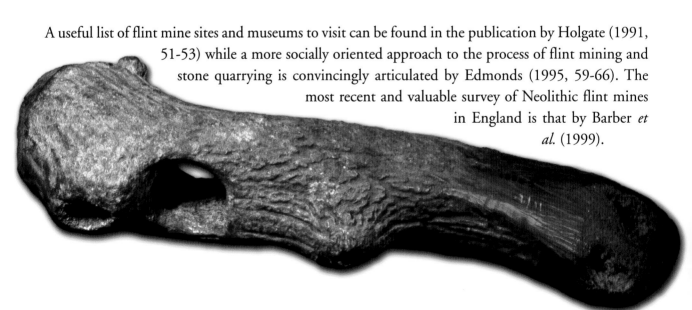

17 - Antler mattock from Willington Quay

2. Stone Tool Manufacture

The Reduction Sequence

Making a stone tool is a skilled and ordered task; it is not something that can be achieved by simply striking a stone at random and hoping the intended shape emerges. Because most stone tool material fractures consistently, the result of each blow can be predicted and knowledge of this allows a nodule to be worked into a specific tool. The steps involved in transforming a lump of stone into a cultural implement follow a set routine which is called the 'reduction sequence' or *chaîne opératoire* (Fig. 18). Tools can be produced in different ways and this means not all reduction sequences follow the same routine. For example, core tools are made by removing flakes from a nodule so that what is left becomes the intended tool, whereas a blade tool is made by preparing a nodule into a shape which allows controlled blanks to be flaked off; the blank is then retouched to make the tool (see Fig. 18). The 'primary' stage of this sequence involves chipping a nodule to prepare a suitable shape ready for detaching further flakes of an intended shape. Waste flakes produced from this process are known as 'primary waste'. The subsequent flaking block is known as a 'core'. Cores are the first part of the 'secondary' stage of the reduction sequence. Flakes are then removed from the core according to the form desired by the flintknapper. This process produces blanks for tool production as well as waste material and core preparation and maintenance flakes. The material resulting from this process is termed 'secondary flakes'. Occasionally secondary flakes of the desired shape are so sharp that they do not require further modification and are used in that form as a tool. The final 'tertiary' stage of the reduction sequence occurs when secondary flakes are either utilised as a tool or further modified to produce an implement. Such additional flaking is termed 'retouch'. Therefore, utilised flakes, retouched flakes, finished implements and the waste chips resulting from their production belong to the tertiary stage of the core reduction sequence. Waste material produced during the various stages of the reduction sequence is sometimes referred to as debitage.

Retouch

A flake can be retouched in a number of different ways. For example, an edge can be retouched in order to blunt it so as to prevent it from cutting the hand when in use. When a blade has one of its long edges intentionally blunted this is referred to as a 'backed blade' (Fig. 19). However, most of the time a flake is retouched in order to create a working edge. This can be achieved in several different ways. 'Steep retouch' (sometimes termed 'abrupt' retouch) refers to flakes that have been retouched at an abrupt angle; such retouch produces an edge invariably between 45 and 90 degrees to the surface from which the blow was applied (Fig. 19). Steep retouch usually, though not always, occurs on just one face of a flake. When only one face of a flake is reworked this type of retouch is termed unifacial and is most commonly associated with Mesolithic and occasional Early Neolithic implements. Invasive retouch refers to flakes that have been retouched at a shallow angle much closer to the horizontal plane (Fig. 19). 'Invasive retouch' is a common characteristic of flake tools from the Palaeolithic onwards and in later prehistoric contexts it is commonly associated with Neolithic and

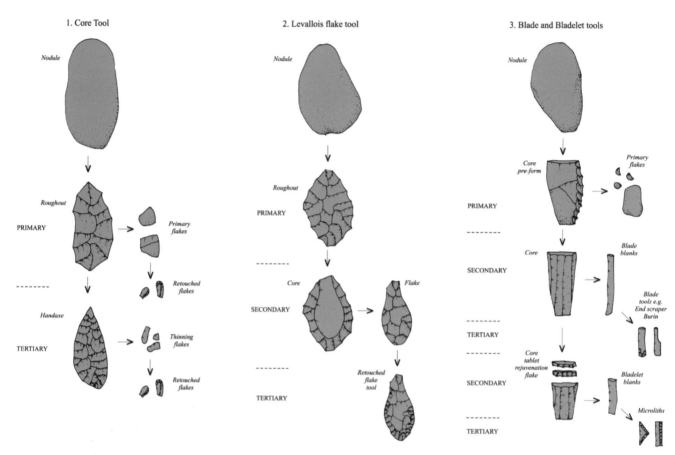

18 - Different types of reduction sequences

Early Bronze Age flintwork though it is absent in Mesolithic traditions. Invasive retouch is frequently applied to both faces of a flake resulting in retouch that is described as bifacial.

A flake can also be retouched by taking out pronounced notches along one side to produce a denticulate (see glossary) while much finer continuous notching can produce a serrated edge. A further method of retouch work is the removal of a burin spall (Fig. 20) which involves striking a blank so as to remove a splinter from it. A burin removal can be either a transverse detachment across the width of the blank or a longitudinal detachment down one side, or part thereof, of a blank. A burin is the name given to the flint implement from which the splinter (burin spall) was detached. Burins are characteristic forms associated with Upper Palaeolithic and Mesolithic manufacturing traditions. Flakes, though more usually blades, can also be modified by the creation of a notch (Fig. 21), either by chipping out an area with several small blows or more typically by pressure flaking (see below). If a flake is lightly sharpened along only a narrow width of its edge/s this is referred to as marginal retouch.

Flake Morphology

All flakes can be described according to universal characteristics. The back of a flake, or the 'dorsal' surface, is the outward facing side of a flake before it was detached from a core or nodule (Fig. 22).

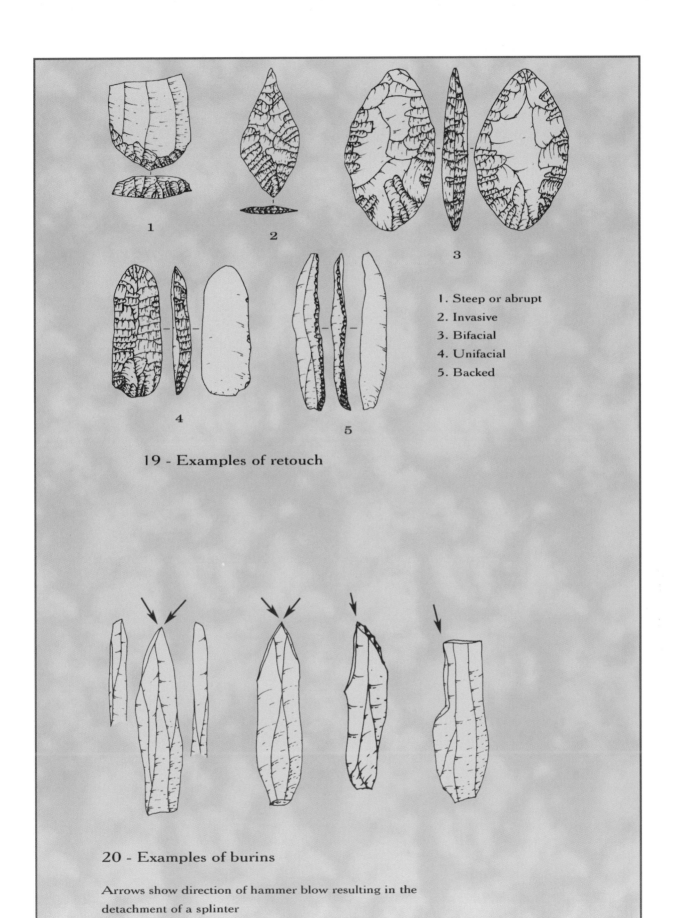

1. Steep or abrupt
2. Invasive
3. Bifacial
4. Unifacial
5. Backed

19 - Examples of retouch

20 - Examples of burins

Arrows show direction of hammer blow resulting in the detachment of a splinter

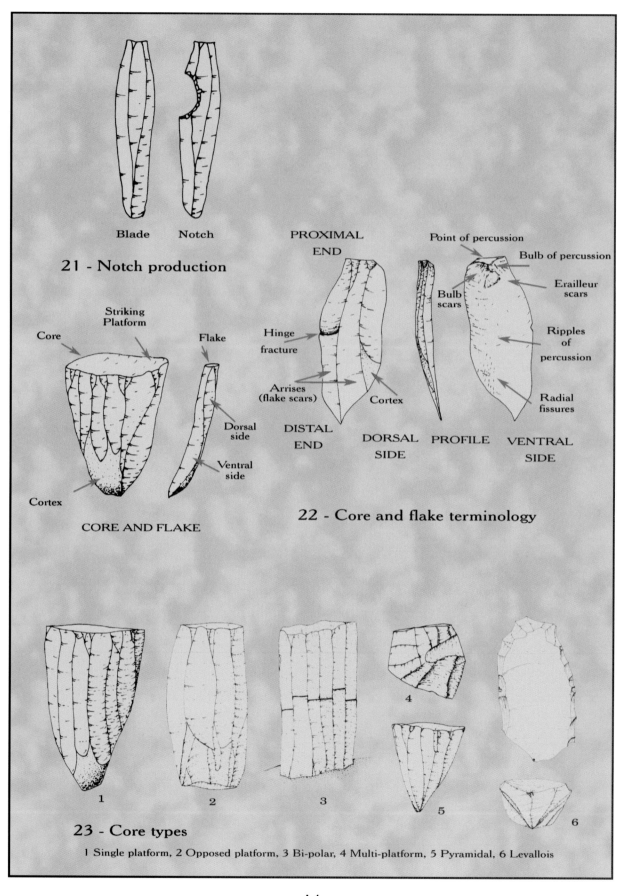

Blade   **Notch**

21 - Notch production

Core

Striking Platform

Flake

Cortex

Dorsal side

Ventral side

CORE AND FLAKE

PROXIMAL END

Point of percussion

Bulb of percussion

Erailleur scars

Bulb scars

Hinge fracture

Ripples of percussion

Arrises (flake scars)

Cortex

Radial fissures

DISTAL END

DORSAL SIDE

PROFILE

VENTRAL SIDE

22 - Core and flake terminology

1

2

3

4

5

6

23 - Core types

1 Single platform, 2 Opposed platform, 3 Bi-polar, 4 Multi-platform, 5 Pyramidal, 6 Levallois

This is usually the irregular side that has flake scars on it. The front of a flake, known as the 'ventral' or 'bulbar' surface, is the inward facing side of a flake before detachment (Fig. 22). This is usually the smooth side, sometimes with traces of a ripple effect on it. These ripples are caused by the shock waves from the conchoidal fracturing of the flake during detachment and are often distinct enough to indicate the direction from which the flake was struck as they tend to radiate outwards in increasingly larger circles from the point of the hammer blow. The end at which a flake was struck in order to detach it from its host piece is called the 'proximal' or 'bulbar' end, while the end opposite this is called the 'distal' end (Fig. 22). The proximal end can often be recognised, not just from the direction and shape of the ripples but also from the occurrence of a 'bulb of percussion' (Fig. 22). Bulbs of percussion can sometimes be extremely slight, leaving a slight bump that can be more easily felt than recognised with the naked eye, while in other cases they can be very exaggerated. Bulbs of percussion tend to vary according to hammer type, as well as between different sources of raw material. Generally, the harder and heavier the hammer the more pronounced the bulb of percussion. They often have a flat top or evidence of crushing if the hammer blow was too heavy.

Core Morphology

Cores come in a wide variety of shapes and forms, but all cores have at least one or more striking platforms. A striking platform is the area or edge where a hammer blow has been applied to the core to detach a flake (Fig. 22). Striking platforms can usually be identified by the flake scars leading from them, slight crushing on the edge caused by the hammer blow or, occasionally, a depression at the top of the flake scars denoting where the bulb of percussion has occurred on the flake. A core platform is usually a flat, flaked surface deliberately produced during the preparation of a core.

Cores are useful for indicating the type of manufacturing techniques that have been employed; for example, whether the production of microliths, parallel-sided blades or squat flakes was intended. Cores have been classified into various types according to the way in which they were utilised for detaching flakes (Fig. 23). A single platform core is the term given to a core that has just one striking platform from which all subsequent flakes and blades were struck. A bi-polar core is the term given to a core that has detachments removed from opposite ends of the piece. These types of cores are typically produced when one end of a core is set on a hard surface, or 'anvil' stone, and then hit on the other end causing a flake to detach from the anvil end. This technique is not common everywhere although it is frequently encountered in northern and western Britain, probably because bipolar technology is appropriate for working small pebbles and is therefore a strategy for coping with a restricted flint supply. As a result, bi-polar cores tend to be smaller than other cores as they allow for more flakes to be extracted and from smaller pieces. Cores that can no longer be flaked are termed 'exhausted cores'. Cores are themselves sometimes subsequently used as tools, such as scrapers. A core that has more than one striking platform that is not opposed is referred to as a multi-directional or multi-platform core (Fig. 23). A Levallois core is the term given to a core that is prepared by producing a Levallois surface (see Fig. 18 and Chapter 3) for the removal of a large piece (Levallois flake). The surface can be prepared again to produce multiple flakes from the core (see Andrefsky 1998, 139-144 for fuller discussion). A large flake, itself utilised as a core for further flake removals, is sometimes referred to as a core flake.

There are various subdivisions of core types that describe those that fall under the general types described above. An example would be the prismatic core, which is a form of single platform core of pyramidal shape, used for detaching blade blanks, usually for microlith production.

Techniques of Manufacture

Stone implements can be produced by flaking, pecking, grinding and polishing, and drilling. Occasionally some lithic materials are heated or soaked in water to improve their workable properties (Mandeville 1973; Patterson and Sollberger 1979; Griffiths *et al* 1987; Olausson 1983), though this is relatively infrequent.

Flaking

Flaking, or knapping, is the method by which chipped stone tools are made. It is an economical and rapid method for producing implements of assorted types. By varying the direction, weight and nature of a controlled hammer blow, the size and shape of the resultant flake can be accurately predicted and these have been classified into four main types: feathered,

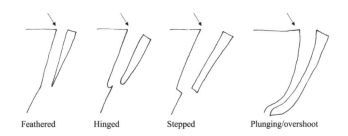

24 - Different types of flake terminations

hinge, stepped and plunging (Fig. 24). The three main forms of flaking are direct flaking, indirect flaking and pressure flaking (Fig. 25). Direct flaking is achieved by striking the nodule/core/flake with a direct blow from a hammer. Wooden hammers are sometimes referred to as 'billets'. The hammer is hand held and can be made from various materials (Fig. 25), each of which produce different results, so a flintknapper would need a range of hammer types at his disposal. Hard hammers include those of flint or quartz (Fig. 27), and medium hammers may be made of sandstone, cortical flint or granite while soft hammers are made from antler, wood or bone. Indirect flaking involves using a punch, placed with the point end on to the area selected for striking. The punch is then struck with a hammer.

Indirect percussion is frequently used for more delicate and controlled work. The punch is typically made from deer antler and used in conjunction with a soft hammer (Fig. 25). Pressure flaking is a precise procedure in which a punch is placed on the required part of the flint and increasing pressure applied until a flake is detached. This is particularly useful for fine retouch work as well as core platform preparation. Pressure flaking is performed using deer antler tines with a pointed or slightly blunted tip (Fig. 25). Recent research has shown that in Denmark small bronze tips were used in some pressure flaking to produce very fine flint copies of bronze daggers (Stafford 1998).

Pecking

Pecking is the term given to the technique of chipping small pieces of rock from its parent. It is a technique that is usually applied to hard stone that does not flake, such as igneous rocks. It is effectively a gradual process of small-scale obliteration, often resulting in a distinctive pocked surface. It is a technique that was employed to help in the preliminary shaping of Group XVIII stone implements such as axe heads, axe-hammers and maces made from Whinstone (quartz dolerite).

Grinding and Polishing

Stone implements are often chipped roughly into shape before they are ground and polished. Classic forms of ground artefacts include flint and stone axe heads (Fig. 28) as well as chisels, knives and scrapers. Grinding is more laborious than flaking but it has the important advantage of being able to produce a stronger working edge or blade. Some artefacts, such as axe heads, are frequently ground all over while others, such as knives and scrapers, are only partially ground, usually along a single or opposed edges. Grinding takes place by rubbing the desired part of the implement along a grinding stone, which may range in size from a large boulder to a hand-held stone. Hand held forms are sometimes referred to as *polissoirs*. Sandstone was probably the most common stone used for grinding. The grinding and polishing of stone tools, like flint mining, was an innovation widely adopted in Britain during the Neolithic period and lasted into the Early Bronze Age. Some Mesolithic ground stone axe heads are known from Wales and Ireland.

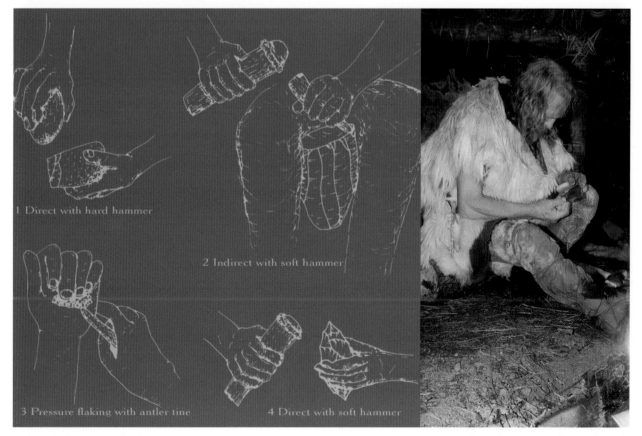

| 25 - Flaking techniques | 26 - Flint knapper John Lord in action |

Drilling

Perforations are achieved by drilling, which is both a cutting and grinding process. When drilling stone, a bit, usually made from a hard sharp material such as flint or bronze, is turned rapidly to cut a hole. No drilling equipment is known for certain but it is often assumed that bow drills were used on the basis of analogies with known primitive technology, such as that used by indigenous American tribes. It is perhaps significant to note that most perforated stone implements make their appearance in Britain at the end of the Late Neolithic and in the Early Bronze Age, and this is the same time that copper metal alloys, and particularly hardened bronze, were adopted.

27 - Hammerstones from northern England. Note the wear visible on some of the facets

28 - Ground and polished stone axe heads from north-east England

3. Palaeolithic Stone Tools

Palaeolithic literally means the 'old stone age'. It refers to the period of human existence up to the end of the last glacial episode, which in the British Isles finished around 12,000 years ago. The Palaeolithic is subdivided into lower, middle and upper phases. The lower Palaeolithic (in the UK) is concerned with the period when the first humans arrived *c.*500,000 years ago to 200,000 years ago, the middle Palaeolithic with the period 200,000 to 40,000 years ago and the upper Palaeolithic with the period 40,000 to 12,000 years ago. Wymer (1999) has recently divided the lower Palaeolithic into a Period 1 and a Period 2 with Period 3 relating to the Middle Palaeolithic (Wymer 1999). It is with the advent of the upper Palaeolithic that anatomically modern humans identical to ourselves first appear in north-west Europe. Archaeological deposits dating from the lower, middle and upper Palaeolithic have been found in Britain although lower and middle Palaeolithic artefacts are rare as subsequent glaciations have swept away most of these remains, particularly in the north.

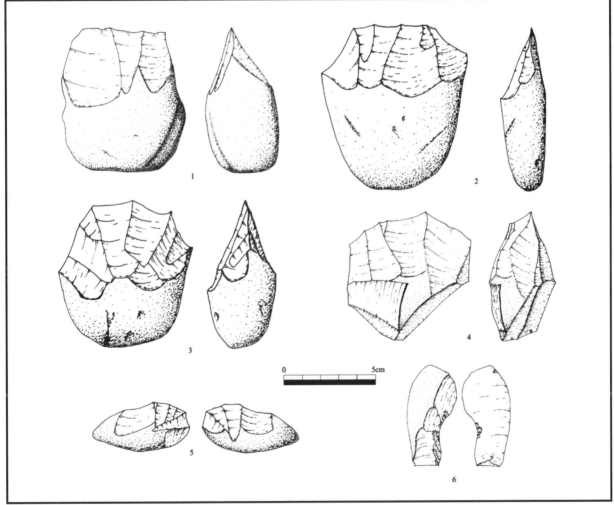

29 - Lower Palaeolithic Clactonian tools.
1 Pebble chopper core, 2 Unifacial chopper, 3 Bifacial chopper, 4 Biconical chopper core,
5 Pebble chopper, 6 Flake tool

Lower Palaeolithic

Important early lower Palaeolithic sites that have produced stone tools include the sites at Boxgrove (Sussex), Clacton-on-Sea (Essex), Swanscombe (Kent) and Barnham St. Gregory (Suffolk). The stone tools utilised during the early phases of the Lower Palaeolithic are based on a crude pebble and flake technology comprising mostly simple pebble choppers, flake tools and utilised cores (Roe 1981; Wymer 1999, and Fig. 29). This type of flaking technology is referred to as the Clactonian tradition, after the assemblages found in ancient river channel deposits at sites around Clacton (Singer *et al.* 1973).

The Clactonian tradition appears to have co-existed with the Acheulian tradition, which is characterised by more elaborate tools including bifacial tools, hand-axes (Fig. 30) and their variants, such as cleavers, as well as scrapers and trimmed flakes

30 - Lower Palaeolithic Acheulian hand axes

(Fig. 31). However, the relationship between these different flaking traditions remains controversial (Wymer 1999, 12).

The hand-axe (Fig. 30) was a heavy multi-purpose tool used as a knife, chopper or pounder. Hand-axes and other bifacial tools are core tools made by reducing a single nodule to produce an implement (see Fig. 18). This is a wasteful method of tool production as all the debitage resulting from the flaking is usually discarded. However, it does allow the knapper to produce large strong tools that can withstand considerable force. These tools are usually symmetrical, bifacially flaked and often trimmed along their entire perimeter.

Important sites which have produced Acheulian stone tools include those at Fordwich, Swanscombe (both Kent), Farnham (Surrey) and Kent's Cavern (Devon). Hand-axes have been found associated with large animals such as horse and rhinoceros at these sites, which has led to them being interpreted as all-purpose butchery tools. They are frequently pointed or ovate and evidence from Boxgrove (Sussex) indicated that axes had been made there using soft hammers of antler. Useful publications concerned with hand-axes include the corpus of finds assembled by Roe (1968a) and more recently the review of Scottish material by Saville (1997). An accessible account of Palaeolithic archaeology, with reference to the stone tool industries, is the short publication by Stuart (1988), while Roe's in-depth work remains a classic (Roe 1981), and the important festschrift to John Wymer, edited by

31- Lower Palaeolithic Acheulian tools
1 Ficron handaxe, 2 Ovate handaxe (redrawn from Barton, 1997), 3, 4 and 5 Scrapers, 6 Cleaver

Ashton *et al* (1998), contains many useful papers by leading experts. Wymer's own recent book contains an excellent overview that covers the earlier stages of the Palaeolithic (Wymer 1999). Useful characterisations of Palaeolithic flint-working traditions can be found in Barton (1997) and Wymer (1999) while Roe's gazetteer still remains a useful reference work regarding the distribution of sites across Britain (1968b).

It is not yet known whether the Clactonian and Acheulian industries represent two different hominid species, two different cultural groups, a chronological development of technology, or different types of tools associated with different functional requirements. The earliest human remains in Britain, consisting of a shin bone and two teeth, have recently been found at Boxgrove (Sussex) associated with an early Acheulian assemblage dating back *c.*500,000 years. Analysis of the fossil remains indicated an adult about 6 feet tall, weighing just over 80kg and likely to be a male. It is thought to belong to the hominid type *Homo heidelbergensis* (see Stringer 1996, for full discussion), which although not fully comparable with modern humans (*Homo sapiens sapiens*), was a more developed type of hominid than *Homo erectus*.

Middle Palaeolithic

The stone tool tradition of the Middle Palaeolithic period is sometimes referred to as the Mousterian, after the rock shelter site of Le Moustier in France, and this is the period associated with *Homo sapiens neanderthalensis* (Neanderthals). There are few remains of this period in the British Isles although human remains and associated lithic artefacts have been discovered at Pontnewyyd cave, North Wales; as a result this period remains poorly understood. The reason for the disappearance of the Neanderthals at the end of this period remains one of the key debates of the later Palaeolithic (Mellars 1996). It is likely that human groups may have abandoned Britain for extended periods during this time, given the alternation between glacial and interglacial conditions.

One defining characteristic of the Mousterian stone tool tradition, however, was the use of some aspects of the 'Levallois' flaking technique (see also Chapter 2). Although the Levallois technique appeared elsewhere in Europe sometime between 200,000 and 100,000 BP, it was not until *c.*100,000 BP that it made its appearance in the British Isles. This technique differed from the Acheulian reductive technology by allowing for the removal of flakes of a predetermined size and shape, sometimes referred to as 'tortoise' flakes because of their oval shape and the pattern of flake removal scars. The

32 - Middle Palaeolithic (Mousterian) tools
1 and 2 Bout Coupé handaxes, 3 Levallois core, 4 Levallois point, 5 Backed blade, 6 Denticulate,
7 Convex side scraper, 8 Transverse scraper, 9 Mousterian point

entire process involved in producing a Levallois flake (see Mellars 1996) could be accomplished using hard hammer percussion (Fig. 32). This intentional production of regular flakes, which could be retouched and made into a variety of flake tools, marks an important advance in early stone tool technology. The Mousterian stone tool industry was based on the production of flakes that were used either as sharp cutting edges or retouched into a restricted range of tools. These include small triangular points, side scrapers, notches, denticulates and the thin flat-based (or *bout coupé*) hand-axes (Barton 1997, 87) (Fig. 32). Use of the Levallois technique and hand-axes continued during the middle Palaeolithic as did the production of various scrapers and bi-faces similar to those of the Acheulian tradition.

Useful references for this period include the pioneering work of Garrod (1926), the volume by Roe (1981) and the important studies of Neanderthals by Stringer (1993) and Mellars (1996).

Upper Palaeolithic

By *c.*40,000 BP modern humans, *Homo sapiens sapiens,* were present in north-west Europe with their arrival recorded in Britain at least as early as *c.*30,000 BP. The lithic technology of the Upper Palaeolithic signals a distinct technological break with preceding periods and is found only in association with modern humans. This period has been subdivided into four successive cultural episodes based on French lithic typologies. Starting with the earliest first, these are the Aurignacian, Gravettian, Solutrean and Magdalenian, the latter also being known as Creswellian in Britain. However, these names are rarely used today by British archaeologists (see for example Smith 1992); instead, the Upper Palaeolithic is usually divided into an early and a late phase. Early Upper Palaeolithic sites in Britain with lithic assemblages are few and are mostly cave sites, such as Creswell Crags (Derbyshire), Kent's Cavern (Devon), Badger's Hole (Somerset) and Paviland Cave (Glamorgan), although occasional open sites have been discovered, such as Barnwood (Gloucestershire). Lithic technology developed significantly in this period, with the hand-axe being replaced by a wider range of tools specifically designed to fulfil particular tasks. This included the adoption of a blade-based technology in place of the previous flake technology whereby narrow blades were struck from prepared cores. Particularly distinctive are the leaf-shaped points and scrapers (Fig. 33) although another characteristic of this period is the range and diversity of tool types made from blades. These include forms of scrapers, piercers, points and burins.

By 25,000 BC the ice sheets started to advance again, reaching their maximum extent ('glacial maximum') around 18,000 BC. During this time most of Britain north of the Bristol Channel was covered by ice and it is likely that much of the country was entirely empty of human occupation, save for occasional hunting visits.

By *c.*15,000 BC the ice sheets were on the retreat, allowing human colonisation to take place once again although several readvances of the ice occurred. The last of these was the Loch Lomond stadial which was over by *c.*10,000 BC. The significant feature of this period is that human settlement was

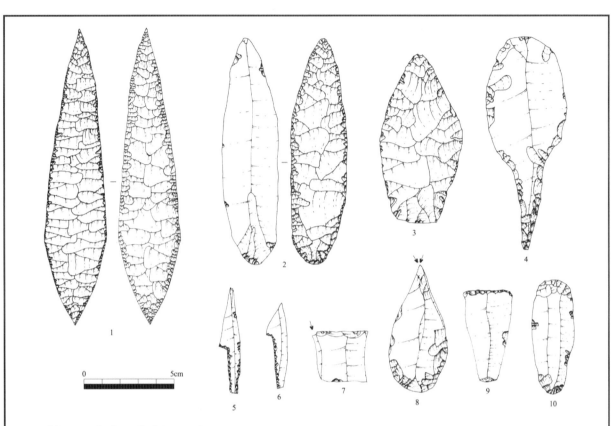

33 - Upper Palaeolithic tools

1 Bifacial Solutrean point, 2 Unifacial Solutrean point, 3 Solutrean point, 4 Tanged point,
5 and 6 Shouldered points, 7 Burin, 8 Composite tool: Burin and end scraper, 9 End scraper,
10 Double end scraper

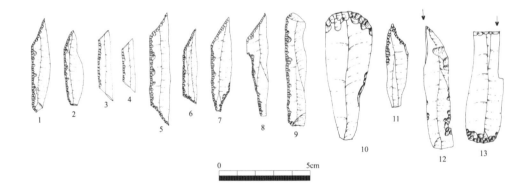

34 - Late Upper Palaeolithic tools

1 and 2 Cresswellian points, 3, 4, 5 and 6 Trapezoidal points, 7 Tanged point, 8 Shouldered point,
9 Backed blade, 10 End scraper, 11 Awl, 12 Burin, 13 Composite tool: Burin and end scraper

not displaced by the glacial readvances and as a result human occupation in Britain has remained unbroken to the present day. This period is conventionally referred to as the Late Upper Palaeolithic.

Late Upper Palaeolithic stone tool assemblages are characterised by distinctive forms (see Campbell 1977 and Barton 1997 for discussions of typologies). These include 'Creswellian' points (Fig. 34), named after the type site of Creswell Crags (see Jenkinson 1984 and Smith 1992, 82-92 for discussion of the site and flint assemblages), along with backed blades, trapezoidal points, 'Cheddar' points, shouldered points and 'penknife' points (Fig. 34). Burins were frequently used during this period and the common form with a chisel-edge is a type of tool thought to have been used to work antler and bone by employing the 'groove and splinter technique' (Fig. 35). It is frequently assumed that there was little, if any, late Upper Palaeolithic occupation beyond the northern borders of Yorkshire and Lancashire; however, a late Upper Palaeolithic tool (Fig. 36) from Tyndedale, Northumberland, has recently been accessioned into the Museum of Antiquities' collection (see Gazetteer entry for Eltringham, Northumberland). The key sites, elsewhere in Britain, which have produced important assemblages of late

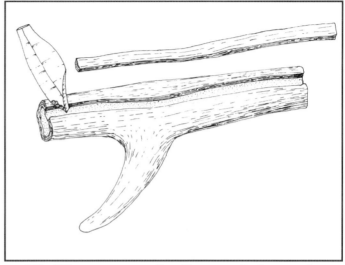

35 - The groove and splinter technique using a burin to produce antler blanks

36 - A Late Upper Palaeolithic blade tool from Tynedale

Upper Palaeolithic flintwork include open sites such as Hengistbury Head (Barton 1992) and cave sites such as those at Cheddar Gorge (see Jacobi 1986 for general account) and Creswell Crags (Jenkinson 1984; Smith 1992, 82-92).

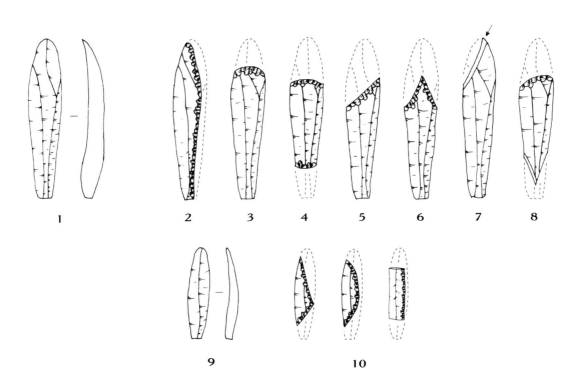

37 - Examples of different tool types made on blades
1 Blade blank, 2 Backed blade, 3 End scraper, 4 Double end scraper, 5 Oblique point, 6 Borer, 7 Burin, 8 Composite tool: end scraper and burin, 9 Bladelet blank, 10 Triangle, crescent and rod microliths (late Mesolithic)

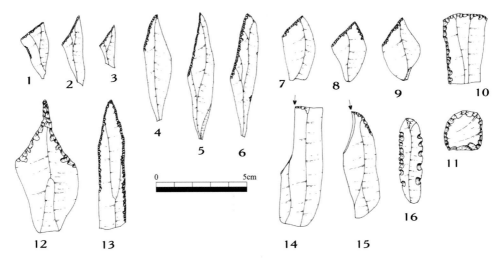

38 - Early Mesolithic tools
1, 2 and 3 Starr Carr type microliths, 4, 5 and 6 Deep Carr type microliths, 7, 8 and 9 Horsham points, 10 and 11 Scrapers, 12 and 13 Awls, 14 and 15 Burins, 16 Saw

4. Mesolithic Stone Tools

In order to allow for comparison with other periods from the Holocene, the dates quoted for the Mesolithic and subsequent periods are given in calibrated radiocarbon years BC. Traditionally scholars who deal with the Mesolithic use uncalibrated radiocarbon years before present (i.e. 1950) whereas scholars dealing with the Neolithic and later periods use calibrated (or calendar) years BC and AD. This creates confusion when dealing with the early and mid Holocene (see glossary) as two different dating schemes are in use that are not immediately comparable. The reason for using calibrated years here is that uncalibrated years bp refer to dates measured from 1950 and not 'before present'; this gap will increase as time goes on as the present is constantly moving. The advantage of using calendar dates BC and AD is that they refer to any given year in time from a fixed point that is widely recognised. As calibration now extends back as far as 22,000 years ago there is no need to continue without calibration for periods since that time.

The Mesolithic, or 'middle stone age', is the name given by archaeologists to the period between the end of the last glaciation (*c.*10,000 BC) and the advent of farming (*c.*4,000 BC). It is conventionally divided into an early and a late period. The early Mesolithic extends from the cool early post-glacial period up to the time when the climate warms up, sea-levels begin to rise and the land bridge between Britain and the continent starts to be inundated *c.*8,000 BC. The late Mesolithic covers the period between *c.*8,000 BC and 4,000 BC.

Early Mesolithic
The Early Mesolithic people of Britain and the lands now under the North Sea inhabited a landscape that underwent considerable change during the Postglacial period. With the dissolution of the ice, the tundra landscape gave way to a land mantled by a patchwork of glacial meltwater lakes and birch-dominated woodland (Smith 1992). Over succeeding millennia the sea level continued to rise, cutting Ireland off from Britain around 8,500 BC, with Britain completely separated from the continent by 6,500 BC, though large islands would have remained in parts of the North Sea perhaps until as late as the end of the Mesolithic. The north-east coastline of Britain, however, extended a little further out to sea than today. The early Holocene drowned forest that survives in peat in the inter-tidal zone at Seaton Carew, Hartlepool, has produced Mesolithic flints (Trechmann 1936) testifying to the presence of early hunter-gatherer populations in areas now drowned by the North Sea. Elsewhere barbed antler points have been dredged up off the Yorkshire coast at Hornsea (Clark and Godwin 1956) and from the Ower and Leman banks in the North Sea (Verhart 1995). Therefore, the Early Mesolithic flint assemblages that are recovered today from the north-east coastal margin should not be seen as representing coastal sites *per se*, but rather, occupation areas along a ridge line that may have comprised the first set of hills on the western edge of the now drowned landmass which formed the North Sea lowlands (see also Coles 1998). As the climate changed during the early Holocene, the British Isles became home to a fully developed mixed deciduous woodland. The period between *c.*7,500 and *c.*5,500 BC is referred to as the 'climatic optimum' because it was during this period that

the most favourable climatic conditions for human occupation were obtained. Average annual temperatures were around 2 degrees Celsius warmer than they are today with longer hours of sunshine and lower annual rainfall. Sea levels continued to rise so that by about 6,500 BC Britain had become an island with broadly the same coastline we have today. However, it must be recognised that much of the east coast of Britain has suffered from extensive erosion since then and considerable tracts of coastline, particularly those with soft sediments, have been lost to the sea and this no doubt accounts for the lack of Mesolithic shell midden sites on the east coast.

It is generally accepted that the Early Mesolithic stone tool kit represents an adaptation to the specific hunting strategies and butchery practices required for the large game animals that inhabited the early Postglacial landscape (e.g. Myers 1989). The stone tools of the Early Mesolithic have many similarities with those of the Late Upper Palaeolithic, being based on a blade technology (Fig. 37) and utilising a similar range of tools, including burins, scrapers, piercers and awls (Fig. 38), as well as tools made from bone and antler. Mesolithic blade tools tend to be made from regular blades struck in a very systematic manner from carefully prepared cores. However, the stone tool that forms the hallmark of the Mesolithic period across Europe is the 'microlith' (meaning 'small stone tool'). Microliths are generally, though not always, points used as barbs in weapons such as spears and arrows. The bow and arrow is thought to have come to prominence during this period as the preferred hunting weapon for the smaller, faster prey associated with the Postglacial environment, such as red deer, roe deer, horse and elk. The larger, slower animals associated with earlier arctic and tundra conditions were probably more easily taken by using spears; bows and arrows may have had difficulty penetrating the flesh of thick-skinned mammoths!

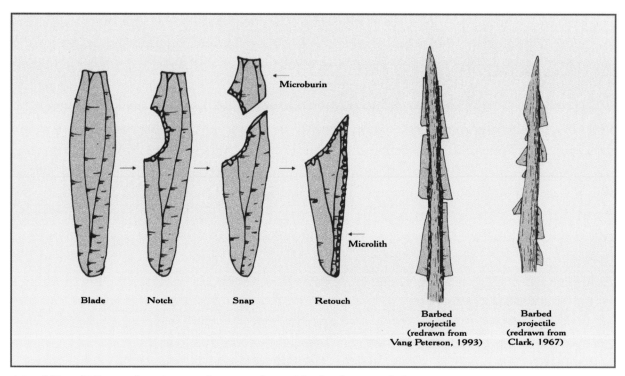

39 - Microlith production and examples of hafted microliths

Microliths, or 'pygmy flints' as they were known to 19th and early 20th century archaeologists, are usually made from broader blade forms during the Early Mesolithic with generally smaller, more narrow-blade forms characterising the Late Mesolithic. Early Mesolithic microliths typically measure between 2 and 4cm in length and include types with oblique blunting across one end (known as 'obliquely blunted points') as well as isosceles triangles and, occasionally, crescents (Fig. 38). The microlith typology for this period is thought to start with Star Carr types, followed by Deep Carr types and then, towards the end of the period, the use of Horsham points (Reynier 1998) (Fig. 38). Microliths were made by chipping out a notch, often at the thicker proximal end of the blade (for greater strength), and then snapping across the notch and trimming along the new edge to produce a sharp tip (Fig. 39). The distinctive waste flake is referred to as a microburin.

Wymer (1991, 15) has suggested that three distinct cultural groups can be identified at the beginning of the Mesolithic in Britain on the basis of his recognition of three different groups of stone tool assemblages. These include (1) assemblages containing long flint blades as well as scrapers and burins with few microliths and no axes, (2) assemblages with an emphasis on shouldered and tanged points, and (3) assemblages containing large numbers of oblique or triangular microliths and usually flint axes. However, these various types of assemblage are not universally acknowledged and such differences that do occur could represent functional variation at different sites or local responses to local conditions, such as scarcity of good quality flint or the need for a tool kit associated with the taking of a specific type of resource, such as fish or birds.

Another distinctive artefact associated with the Early Mesolithic tool kit is the tranchet-axe, which takes its name from the final transverse flake removed across the blade end to produce a sharp cutting edge (Fig. 40). Such axes could be easily resharpened by detaching a new flake by another transverse blow. Few, if any, tranchet axe heads have been retrieved from secure Late Mesolithic contexts and it appears that they are associated with Early Mesolithic traditions.

The best known Early Mesolithic site in Britain is that at Star Carr in the Vale of Pickering, Yorkshire (Clark 1954). Nearly 17,000 flints were discovered during the excavations including scrapers, microliths, awls, burins and axes. One of the microliths retained on its surface traces of resin that had been used to glue the barb into a shaft. A flint assemblage of a similar size and composition has also been found at the Late Upper Palaeolithic-Early Mesolithic river gravel terrace site at Thatcham, Berkshire (Wymer 1962). An important

40 - Examples of two tranchet axes
Blade formed by single flake detachment

group of upland sites that have produced assemblages of Early Mesolithic date are those in the southern Pennines, such as those at Deepcar (Radley and Mellars 1964), Warcock Hill (Radley *et al* 1974) and Lominot (*ibid*; and see also Smith 1992 for discussion). At these sites flint that had come from a source area over 80km away in East Yorkshire was used in the production of hunting weapons, indicating the extensive range of movement in the routines of Postglacial hunters of the south Pennine uplands.

41 - A biserial antler harpoon from Whitburn

Although flint artefacts were the mainstay of the Early Mesolithic tool kit, it is worthy of note that antler and bone tools also formed a significant component in both the Late Upper Palaeolithic and Early Mesolithic toolbox. Uniserial (barbed along one side) and biserial (barbed along both sides) antler points were made, with uniserial points common on earlier sites and biserial points more common in later contexts, though this is only a general trend as both types of harpoons can be found in both periods. Figure 41 shows an example of a biserial harpoon in the Museum of Antiquities' collection which was found on the shore at Whitburn, Tyne and Wear, in 1852 (Mellars 1970), and may well have been washed in from a submerged Mesolithic ground surface situated off the modern coastline. A similar biserial harpoon has been found more recently on the shore of the Forth estuary (Saville 2001), again testifying to earlier Mesolithic activity in the lowland basin now occupied by the North Sea.

Late Mesolithic

The stone tool kit of the hunter-gatherers of the Late Mesolithic was still based on a blade technology although a number of diagnostic traits characterise the implements of this period. Microliths are usually made from narrower blades than in the Early Mesolithic and they are often smaller with distinctive geometric forms (Fig. 42) including backed blades, points, scalene triangles, crescents and towards the end of the Late Mesolithic rectangular shapes known as 'rods' (Figs. 43 and 44). Some types were specific to particular areas, such as the hollow-based points of the Weald. At the Howick site on the Northumberland coast, an important assemblage of flints was acquired from within a well-preserved Mesolithic hut. Dating to *c*.7,800 BC (Cal.) at the beginning of the Late Mesolithic, the

42 - The contrast between broad blade (lower) and narrow blade (upper) microliths

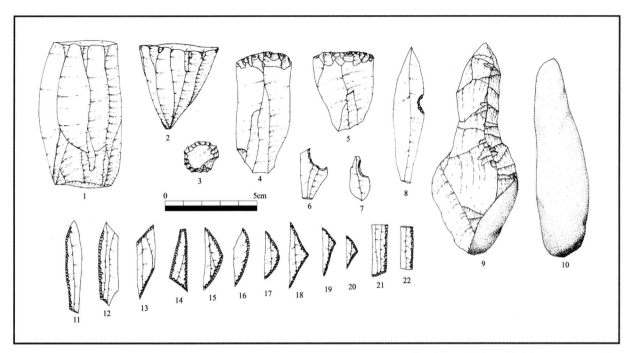

43 - Late Mesolithic stone tools
1 Opposed platform core, 2 Pyramid core, 3 Tiny Scraper, 4 and 5 End scrapers, 6 and 7 Microburins,
8 Notched blade, 9 Pick, 10 Bevelled tool, 11- 22 Microliths, 11 and 12 Backed blades,
13 and 14 Geometrics, 13, 16 and 17 Crescents, 18 Isoceles triangle, 19 and 20 Scalene trangles,
21 and 22 Rods

microlith component was dominated by scalene triangles although backed blades, crescents, isosceles triangles, needle points and some unusual 'thick-edged' microliths were also present.

The Late Mesolithic stone tool assemblage collected during the author's fieldwalking programme in the Milfield Basin, Northumberland, comprised over 50% non-flint lithic material that was derived from local sources, including agate, chert and quartz (Fig. 45). All the diagnostic flint recovered during the recent excavation of the Mesolithic settlement at Howick on the Northumberland coast was either beach or glacial flint that could be picked up in the immediate environs of the site. This heavy reliance on local materials during the period has led a number of archaeologists to consider that there was a reduction in the extent of mobility across the landscape relative to the Early Mesolithic period when people are thought to have roamed more widely (see above). The lithic assemblages from nearby Tweeddale and its tributary valleys on the Scottish side of the Border show a similar composition to the Milfield assemblage, with local agates and cherts found in the river gravels being commonly used (Mulholland 1970). It would seem, then, that in the north-east there was a significant degree of reliance on local materials during the Late Mesolithic, with some higher quality flint imported from distant sources such as the grey speckled flint from north-east Yorkshire. A similar scenario is evident in other areas of northern Britain; for example, the stone tools recovered from the excavation of Mesolithic deposits on the Isle of Rhum produced a stone tool assemblage in which the local bloodstone comprised over 50% of the assemblage (Wickham-Jones 1990) while the chipped stone tools recovered during fieldwalking around Strath Tay were made almost exclusively from local quartz (Bradley 1995).

44 - Late Mesolithic narrow blade microliths from Howick, Northumberland

45 - Microliths made from non-flint materials from the Milfield Basin, Northumberland: banded agate, chert, quartz

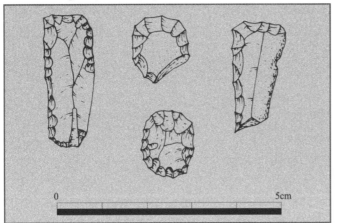

46 - Late Mesolithic scrapers from Howick with abrupt retouch

Another characteristic feature of Mesolithic flint technology is the use of abrupt retouch, particularly common on tool types such as scrapers (Figs. 46 and 47). The end-scraper, where the retouched scraping edge is located at one end of a blade, often the thicker proximal end, was also popular during this period (Fig. 47). Other distinctive forms include cores with blade scars formed by the production of narrow bladelets for subsequent microlith production. These cores often acquire a pyramidal shape making them easy to identify. A method of flaking blades from cores which became widespread during this period, particularly in northern Britain, was the use of bipolar flaking (see Chapter 2), although, like end scrapers and other blade forms, its use continued into the Early Neolithic.

Important new discoveries have been the Mesolithic sites discovered on the north-east coast at Howick (Fig. 48), Northumberland (Waddington *et al* 2003) and at East Barns near Dunbar (John Gooder pers comm.), Fife Ness (Wickham-Jones and Dalland 1998) and Cramond (Saville pers comm.) in Scotland. These sites, though producing Late Mesolithic narrow blade material, have been radiocarbon-dated to the centuries between *c.*7,500 and 8,000 BC (Cal.) making them the earliest Late Mesolithic sites so far discovered in the region. The Fife Ness and Cramond sites are understood to be short-stay camps, with evidence of hearths and small shelters, where the repair of hunting tools, particularly crescentic microliths in the case of Fife Ness, took place. The Howick and Dunbar sites are altogether more substantial sites and include the remains of well-made circular huts, thought to be dwellings, supported by wooden posts, with occupation at Howick lasting over several centuries. Both sites produced thousands of flints, with microliths, scrapers, awls, burins and a wide range of retouched blades and flakes. Tool manufacture at both sites relied on a narrow blade tradition with bipolar flaking of the small beach pebble flints a common characteristic. These sites provide substantive evidence that human groups were occupying the north-eastern coast of Britain north of

47 - Late Mesolithic scrapers from Howick

Yorkshire during the Early Mesolithic-Late Mesolithic interface at a time when rising sea-levels were drowning large areas of the North Sea plain. In addition, the precision dating of the hearth sequence through the three phases of the hut at the Howick site demonstrates that this sequence of structures was used for well over a hundred years. This indicates use of the structure by several generations of what was presumably the same family group, together with a greater degree of permanency in certain parts of the landscape than has previously been thought.

Wymer's (1991) short book on the Mesolithic provides a good starting point for the first time reader while more specialist papers by active researchers can be found in the volumes edited by Bonsall (1989), Ashton *et al* (1998) and Young (2000). These latter publications, together with the important book by Smith (1992), contain many of the key references necessary to pursue further research into lithics and the Mesolithic period.

48 - The excavated Mesolithic settlement at Howick, Northumberland

51 - (photo) A stone axe head in facsimile haft (Museum of Antiquities) and inset
50 - Axe found with surviving haft from Ehenside Tarn (Cumbria) (Ehenside Tarn redrawn from Darbishire, 1874)

5. Early Neolithic Stone Tools

In the centuries around 4000 BC significant changes occurred in the way people lived in, and related to, the world around them, although there were many strands of continuity from the preceding Mesolithic (Bradley 1998; Whittle 1996; Waddington 2000). The beginning of the Neolithic is often equated with the onset of farming, but this is probably too narrow a definition as it fails to acknowledge the transformations in ideology that were also central to the change in lifestyle represented by the Neolithic. The ambiguities which are therefore inherent in the Early Neolithic period, characterised by aspects of change and continuity, are particularly visible in the character of its stone tool kit.

In the Neolithic, radical innovations can be observed in flaking technology, artefact form and in the methods of acquisition of raw materials. The method of grinding and polishing chipped stone tools became widespread, with artefacts such as ground and polished stone axe heads (Fig. 49), chisels and adzes replacing the flaked axe heads of the Mesolithic. Stone axe heads, which form an entire subject of study in their own right, were made from a wide variety of fine-grained stone sources. Many of these stone types had not been previously exploited, including in particular those from volcanic sources in northern and western Britain. Two fine examples of ground and polished stone axe heads found with their wooden hafts are those from Ehenside Tarn, Cumbria (Darbishire 1874), and Shulishader, Scotland. An interpreted facsimile of a hafted stone axe can also be seen on display in the Museum of Antiquities (Fig. 51). For further discussion of the nature and types of stone axe heads the two volumes edited by Clough and Cummins (1979 and 1988) provide the obvious starting point, while there are useful discussions

49 - Neolithic ground and polished stone axes from Kyloe Crags, Blenkinsop and Kielder

concerned with the significance of stone axe heads in Edmonds (1995), Pitts (1996) and Cooney (1998). The most recent discussion concerning exchange networks, together with the results of survey and excavation at the Langdale axe-factory sites, is that by Bradley and Edmonds (1993).

Another technological development that became increasingly favoured as the Neolithic progressed was the use of invasive rather than steep retouch. New forms characteristic of this period which were made using invasive techniques include the leaf-shaped arrowhead (Fig. 52) and the laurel-leaf form, which

52 - Examples of leaf-shaped arrowheads from the Scottish Borders

is thought to have been used as a knife, or possibly a spear point (Fig. 53). Some leaf-shaped arrowheads were evidently made in haste and such types are commonly found during fieldwalking; however, many of the finer examples have come from burial contexts where they were deposited as grave goods. Some of the more exquisite arrowheads come in distinctive forms such as the tear-drop, kite shape and ogival arrowheads. It has been noted by several commentators that leaf-shaped arrowheads are frequently found associated with Late Mesolithic flint scatters, which may be evidence of continuity in the spatial distribution and settlement mobility of Late Mesolithic and Early Neolithic groups (e.g. Bradley 1978; Young 1989; Edmonds 1995). This is a pattern which has been seen in the north-east at Low Shilford near Corbridge (Weyman 1980), around Sandyford Quarry Field near Bolam Lake (Waddington and Davies 2002, Fig. 54), and by the author's fieldwalking programme across the Milfield Basin (Waddington 1999a). However, due to the coarse chronology of fieldwalking assemblages, the presence of Mesolithic pieces and Early Neolithic pieces on the same site should not necessarily be assumed to indicate direct continuity of settlement or land-use as this oversimplifies the process by

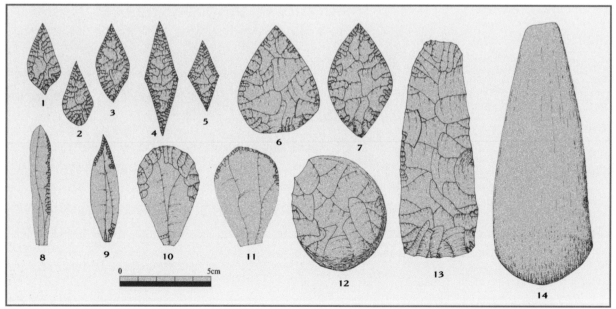

53 - Early Neolithic tools
1, 2 and 3 Leaf shaped points, 4 and 5 Lozenges, 6 and 7 Laurel leaves, 8 Backed blade, 9 Piercer, 10 and 11 End scrapers, 12 Edge polished knife, 13 Flint axe, 14 Ground and polished stone axe

which lithic scatters form over time. Indeed the Mesolithic occupation of an area and subsequent Early Neolithic activity may be separated by perhaps thousands of years.

The range of tools in production during this period also expanded and included implements such as invasively retouched sickles (Fig. 55), thought to have been used for the processing of domesticated plant foods, such as emmer wheat and barley which are known to have been harvested across the British Isles at this time. This expansion in the tool kit probably reflects the wider range of tasks that were being undertaken in association with the tending of domestic plants and animals.

54 - Excavations on the Neolithic settlement at Bolam Lake, Northumberland

Overall, the main features of the Early Neolithic stone tool manufacturing tradition are an increase in the variety of implements being produced, a change in sourcing to include large-scale flint mining and stone quarrying, the use of new techniques such as grinding, polishing and invasive retouch, and a

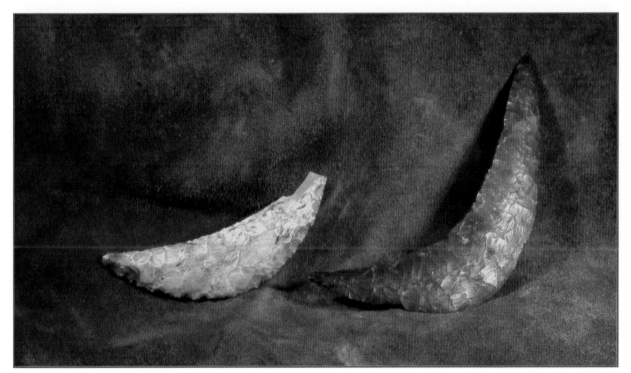

55 - Invasively flaked sickles typical of the Neolithic. Examples pictured are from Denmark

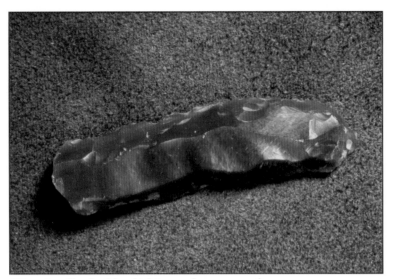

56 - An Early Neolithic end scraper from the Milfield Basin

more widespread use of pressure flaking, while at the same time there was still a reliance on the same basic narrow blade technology which characterised the Late Mesolithic period. Among the artefact types that survived were end scrapers (Fig. 56) and platform cores for the production of blades. Many types of unretouched, retouched and serrated blade tools are found in Early Neolithic assemblages (Fig. 57) with retouch frequently along most of their edges. It is perhaps significant that the main implements which changed between the Late Mesolithic and Early Neolithic periods were those which were generally held to have been of most symbolic value, that is, arrowheads, axe heads and cutting tools such as knives. The symbolic and ritual connotations of stone axe heads are evidenced by their intentional deposition in ceremonial and dedicatory contexts in and around early Neolithic enclosures, burial mounds and other ceremonial monuments in pits and ditch fills.

57 - Early Neolithic blade tools from the Milfield Basin, Northumberland

For example, an important cache of stone axe heads was found buried in what is understood to be a section of ditch in a resident's garden at Heddon-on-the-Wall in Northumberland (Burgess 1984, 140; Sockett 1971). The symbolic power ascribed by modern-day indigenous groups to arrowheads, which have the power to penetrate through flesh and draw the life blood from living things, has also been brought to attention by the ethnographic research of Taçon (1991).

Following on from this, it has been argued that changes evident in the Early Neolithic stone tool kit were primarily associated with the changing meanings associated with the key symbolic aspects of the tool kit, namely cutting tools such as axe heads, arrowheads and knives, rather than with an overhaul of the basic technology which still remained a largely blade-based industry (Waddington 2000). It can also be argued that the new manufacturing methods (namely grinding and polishing and the use of invasive retouch) ensured that stone tools took on a more 'acculturated' appearance. By this it is meant that these forms no longer showed obvious signs of the natural origin of the material from which they were made. As a result these forms take the appearance of overtly human objects. It is, therefore, suggested that these new methods were as much about ways of producing explicitly 'man-made' objects, which separated them from their natural origins by means of their visual appearance and production technique, as they were innovations in stone tool technology. The notion of changes in symbolic tool types relating to changes in meaning and beliefs has also been argued for other areas of north-west Europe (Stafford 1999).

Important publications which deal with aspects of Early Neolithic stone tool industries include the discussion on waste flakes by Pitts and Jacobi (1979) and the analysis of arrowhead forms by Green (1980), while there are many useful papers in the volumes edited by Brown and Edmonds (1987) and Brooks and Phillips (1989), as well as the important volume *Stone Tools and Society* by Edmonds (1995). There are also many relevant sections in the excavation reports from various Early Neolithic sites, such as those on Hazleton North long cairn (Saville 1990), the Staines causewayed enclosure (Robertson-Mackay 1987), Carn Brea (Saville in Mercer 1981a) and the Hambledon Hill excavations (Mercer 1980). A particularly useful summary article is the recent paper discussing flint assemblages from Early Neolithic enclosures by Saville (2002). There are also many helpful articles in the journal *Lithics* that deal with aspects of Early Neolithic flintwork.

58 - Later Neolithic side scrapers from Thirlings

59 - Early Bronze Age thumbnail scrapers from the Scottish Borders

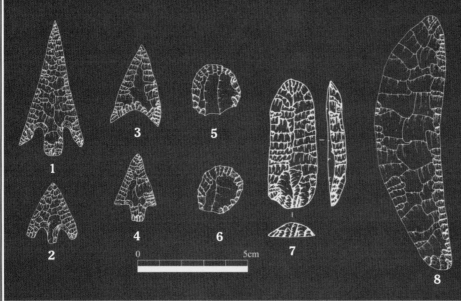

60 - Late Neolithic-Early Bronze Age tools
1 and 2 Barbed and tanged arrowheads,
3 Barbed/hollow-based arrowhead,
4 Tanged arrowhead,
5 and 6 Thumbnail scrapers,
7 Plano-convex knife,
8 Sickle

6. Late Neolithic and Early Bronze Age Stone Tools

The Late Neolithic and Early Bronze Age have been included together in this section as many of the stone tool forms overlap between these periods and are part of the same manufacturing tradition. It covers the period from approximately 3200-1500 BC.

Around 3200 BC, the time at which the Late Neolithic conventionally begins, significant developments took place ranging from the widespread adoption of henge monuments and changes in the settlement pattern to the proliferation of new styles of material culture. The latter included new kinds of highly decorated ceramics, such as Grooved Ware, as well as distinctive stone tool types.

Many of the characteristics that developed during the Early Neolithic became more pronounced by Late Neolithic times, with invasive retouch and edge-polished tools becoming increasingly common, and tool manufacture shows a preference towards large irregular flakes rather than a blade-based industry (see for example Clark 1932; 1934a; Healy 1984; Edmonds 1995). Flaking techniques became more varied to include the production of some of the most exquisite tools (for display and ceremonial purposes) on the one hand, as well as roughly worked pieces for day-to-day use on the other. For the latter, more mundane tools there are fewer defining characteristics that allow them to be recognised. The rougher flaking practices may, in part, be a response to increased access to raw materials and, therefore, less need for maintaining a more sparing blade-based technology. It may also represent a response to a reduction in mobility and therefore less need for a light, mobile, blade-based tool kit. In Northumberland there is a decline in the use of poorer quality, locally available materials in favour of higher quality, imported flint that was evidently exchanged over considerable distances.

61 - A plano-convex knife showing the convex surface from Stargate, Ryton

Typically, cores are of the multidirectional and irregular varieties, while flakes are generally larger and struck with less concern for pursuing a set flaking strategy than in the Early Neolithic. End scrapers made on blades become less common as squat side scrapers increased in popularity (Figs. 58 and 60), together with the sub-circular, invasively retouched, thumbnail scrapers frequently found in burial contexts associated with beakers (Fig. 59 and 60). In Yorkshire, finely made edge-ground scrapers were produced. Crudely-made borers, scrapers and notched tools are also common in the Early Bronze Age (Fig. 60), usually made on flakes which show little evidence for anticipating or avoiding errors during the flaking process.

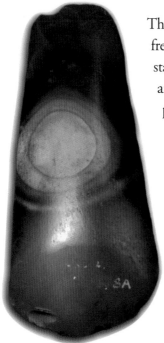

The stone tools that seem to have carried symbolic significance, and which are frequently found in ceremonial contexts, were made to an altogether different standard. These fine lithics include types of barbed and tanged arrowheads, an array of transverse arrowheads, plano-convex knives (Fig. 61) discoidal and polished knives (Fig 60), thumbnail scrapers, elaborate ground and polished flint axe heads (Figs. 62 and 63) and adze blades, perforated maceheads and carved stone balls. Fine, invasively flaked implements such as chisels and daggers (Fig. 64 and 65) were also produced. Some flint daggers were probably never intended for practical use while others have edge damage demonstrating a utilitarian function. These flint daggers bear striking similarities to the early copper and bronze daggers that also make their appearance in the archaeological record at the same time as the beaker and it is clear that they represent the emulation of metal tools in flint form (Fig. 64 and 65).

62 - A ground and polished flint axe head from Morpeth that indicates careful selection of an attractively patterned nodule

These special pieces do not appear to have been in common circulation but rather reserved for display, ceremony and disposal in votive settings or in the graves of important individuals. For example, Harding's excavations on the Milfield North henge produced six fine barbed and tanged arrowheads (Fig. 66, see gazetteer entry for Milfield henge sites), of which five, all in the same honey-grey flint, were recovered from pit VIII (Harding 1981, 115). Thumbnail scrapers (Fig. 67) and barbed and tanged arrowheads are frequently found with 'beaker burials', although they also occur as grave goods in other Early

Bronze Age burial contexts. However, on occasions less exotic lithic artefacts were also placed in burials, such as the seven roughly worked flints and two flint nodules that came out of a beaker from a cist burial at the Sneep, Bellingham (Fig. 68, see gazetteer entry for Bellingham). Elsewhere, at Haugh Head near Wooler a food vessel burial was discovered together with a flint spearhead and oblique arrowhead (Fig. 69, see gazetteer entry for Wooler).

63 - Two finely made flaked and edge-ground flint axe heads from the Cheviots and Budle Bay

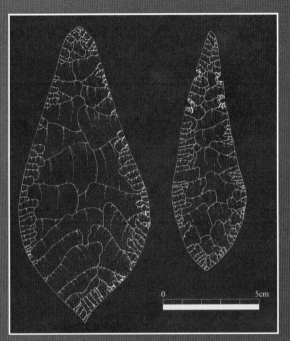

64 - Late Neolithic-Early Bronze Age flint daggers.

65 - Flint daggers, probably copies of metal daggers (Denmark)

66 - A cache of barbed and tanged arrowheads from the Milfield North henge

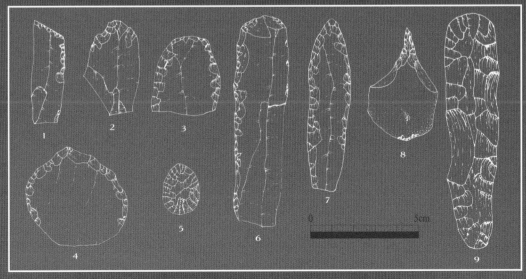

67 - Early Bronze Age tools 1 and 2 Retouched flakes, 3 End scraper, 4 Side scraper, 5 Thumbnail scraper, 6 and 7 Knives, 8 Borer, 9 Fabricator

68 - A beaker with accompanying flints from The Sneep, Bellingham

69 - A food vessel with accompanying flint spearhead and oblique arrowhead from a cist burial at Haugh Head, Wooler

A distinctive range of arrowheads, departing from the earlier leaf-shaped form, characterised the Late Neolithic-Early Bronze Age period. These include the *petit-tranchet* derivative forms, 'chisel' arrowheads and oblique arrowheads (Figs. 70 and 71) that come into use in the later Neolithic. There is little regional variation in these forms, save for the finely made ripple-flaked oblique arrowheads that are particularly common in east Yorkshire and in ceremonial contexts elsewhere around the country. The main group of arrowhead forms characteristic of the Early Bronze Age period are barbed and tanged arrowheads (Fig. 72 and 73) and their variants. Although barbed and tanged arrowheads are often very finely made from flint that appears to have been specially selected for its striking visual appearance, these arrowhead forms can, on occasion, also be quite crude and made from unprepossessing flint flakes. The latter types appear to have been intended for utilitarian purposes whereas the more exquisite, symmetrical and delicate forms are often recovered from graves, votive pits and other special settings, indicating that their purpose was more symbolic than functional. Moreover, most of the latter pieces show absolutely no sign of ever having been used, being freshly chipped and in pristine condition, further implying a non-functional role.

Artefacts comprising the 'Beaker Package'	
Beaker	Barbed and Tanged Arrowheads
Thumbnail Scrapers	V-Perforated Buttons
Archer's Wristguards	Bronze Riveted Daggers
Maceheads	Gold Earrings

Although essentially a north-east Scottish phenomenon, carved stone balls are another form of lithic object that, although not regarded as functional, was used in the Neolithic period both on settlements and ceremonial sites. They are generally thought to have possessed symbolic and/or ritual qualities although their actual purpose remains a mystery (see Edmonds 1992 for discussion). Examples are occasionally found elsewhere in Britain, such as the carved stone ball from Hetton North Farm, Lowick, Northumberland (Speak and Aylett 1996), and the stone ball from Houghton-le-Side

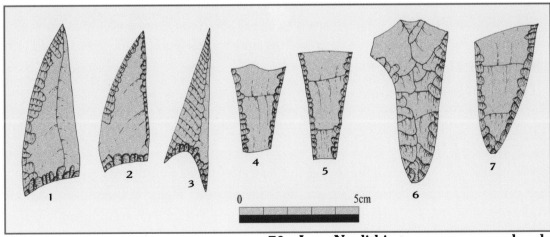

70 - Late Neolithic transverse arrowheads
1 and 2 Oblique points, 3 Ripple-flaked oblique point, 4 and 5 Petit-tranchet arrowheads,
6 and 7 Chisel heads

Clockwise:

71 - Oblique arrowheads, central example with an unusual notch; from Thirlings

72 - Barbed and tanged arrowheads from various sites in Northumberland

73 - Barbed and tanged arrowheads from the Scottish Borders

near Bishop Auckland, County Durham (Fig. 74) in the Museum of Antiquities' collection. A good starting point for the further study of carved stone balls is the publications by Marshall (1977; 1983) which provide a corpus of all the known finds.

Perforated maceheads are one of the most attractive stone implement types of this period (Fig. 75), although the earliest examples appear to have been made from antler, such as those discovered at Duggleby Howe, Yorkshire and Liff's Low, Derbyshire (see Simpson 1996 for recent discussion of antler maceheads). Maceheads are thought to have been made by chipping out the rough shape and then carefully grinding down the surface until the required highly polished finish, and sometimes relief decoration, was achieved. Many of the stone sources used for the production of stone axe heads were also utilised for the production of maceheads. In north-east England they were made of whinstone as well as other pebble and erratic material. Frequently found in burial contexts, maceheads appear to have been prestige objects that may have been used as symbols of authority and/or powerful objects for use in conducting ritual, while others may have been used as weapons or hammers.

Another distinctive hallmark of the latest stages of the Neolithic and Early Bronze Age are the perforated stone implements known as axe hammers and battle axes. They are symmetrical along their long axis and vary in shape from short and stubby to long and thin. The very finely made examples, such as that pictured in Fig. 76, were probably prestige objects for display purposes only that were intended to convey the status of their owner. Others, however, are more crudely made (Fig. 77) and show clear signs of use. Axe hammers and battle axes are made from a wide variety of non-flint stone types, including the whinstone of north-eastern England (Group XVIII, see Clough and Cummins 1988) as well as other dolerites, greywackes and quartzites. Although early examples of battle axes were probably used in warfare, the more elaborate later types probably had a more symbolic role. Battle axes are usually found as grave goods in male graves, presumably to convey the martial power of the deceased man, while axe hammers are rarely found in such contexts and have notably few associations with formal deposits, implying that their significance/use lay in a different sphere. The difference between the two types is entirely dependent on size, with the smaller examples, able to be wielded one-handed, known as battle axes and the more massive larger pieces termed axe-hammers. An interesting anecdote was recalled by a butcher from Corbridge who donated an axe-hammer to the Museum (Fig. 78). Although he had used it as a doorstop his father had, in years gone by, used it to slaughter cattle for beef. It certainly seems tempting to consider how far back this practice may go.

74 - The carved stone ball from Houghton-le-Side, County Durham

75 - A battle axe from Newcastle and macehead from Wallington

76 - An example of a fine, and apparently unused, battle axe from Northumberland

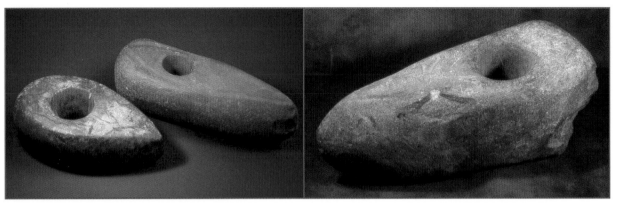

77 - Typical battle axes with evidence of use; from Whickham and Gunnerton

78 - An axe-hammer from Corbridge

Flint mines continued to be used into the Early Bronze Age, indicating that the supply of high quality nodular flint in significant quantities remained important. However, there was still a reliance on locally available materials, particularly in areas of Scotland where quartz and other materials continued to be used. Flint flakes and artefacts from earlier periods were frequently re-used reflecting, it seems, an opportunistic recycling strategy in these areas. Although many of the utilitarian stone tools were made in a somewhat slapdash fashion, and may have been made as and when required, the extremely fine elaborate types may have been made by specialist craftsmen.

With the advent of metal and its widespread circulation by the later stages of the Early Bronze Age, the value of stone objects as prestige goods is thought to have lapsed (see Edmonds 1995), having been replaced by fine objects made from gold, bronze, jet and amber (Fig. 79). However, the advent of

79 - A selection of amber discs, gold jewellery and a jet necklace spacer, typical of Early Bronze Age high status burials in Northumberland

metal technology demanded new resources, particularly copper and tin ore. This led to a new kind of mining that took place while flint mines were still being exploited. Copper mining followed mineral seams and good examples of Early Bronze Age workings include Alderly Edge in Cheshire and the Great Orme mines in North Wales. Associated with these mineral workings was a new range of tools that included a type of stone hammer used for battering the wall face, though this was often employed after fire-setting had been used to crack the stone. These tools are termed 'mauls' and can be identified by the groove running around the tool with a bulbous head at one end and a wedge-shaped head at the other (Fig. 80).

80 - Two stone mauls: tools associated with copper mining; from West Chilton and Green Leighton

Many site reports contain well produced catalogues and discussions of flintwork dating to this period, such as the monographs on the Mount Pleasant (Wainwright 1979, 139-163) and Durrington Walls henges (Wainwright and Longworth 1971), while the book edited by Clarke *et al* (1985) contains a series of beautifully produced photographs of the more elaborate examples of Late Neolithic and Early Bronze Age stonework. The book by Edmonds (1995) contains a series of chapters that discuss the changing nature of lithic artefact production over this period in relation to their contexts of use and deposition, and introduces the reader to a web of social relations that may have been embodied in the use, exchange and production of stone tools. The article by Ford *et al* (1984) discusses the relationship between later flintwork and the emergence of metalworking in Britain.

Later Use of Stone Tools

Although some specialists still maintain that stone tools were no longer used after the widespread adoption of metal by the later Bronze Age (Saville 1981b), there is evidence to suggest that stone tools went on being used during the Late Bronze and Iron Age. Recent papers by Young and Humphrey (1999) and Humphrey and Young (1999), which draw on previous studies by Clarke and Fell (1953), Martingell (1988) and Robins (1996), have discussed the argument for this later use of flint in an effort to stimulate research and debate on the subject. Attention is drawn to the flint assemblages found on Late Bronze Age and Iron Age sites that are usually dismissed as residual but which they believe to be contemporary with the Late Bronze Age-Iron Age occupation. They have also recognised a pattern in the forms of lithic artefacts in these assemblages. The characteristics include the use of highly localised raw materials - some of very poor quality - small assemblages, simple flake technology employing hard hammer direct percussion, a lack of knapping skills, a restricted range of formal tool types, crude hammerstones, a predominance of secondary flakes and the possible recycling of lithic material.

81 - Examples of gun flints

Later still, of course, is the use of flints in early musketry pieces. These 'gun flints' (Fig. 81) were used to create the spark in rifles such as the flintlock (Fig. 82). Also used as a building material in East Anglia, Sussex and elsewhere, and as a constituent of Wedgwood pottery, flint is occasionally used today by surgeons when making incisions into flesh. The advantage over the modern surgical scalpel

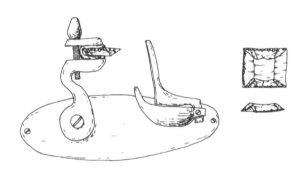

82 - The positioning of a gun flint in a musket mechanism (redrawn from Whittaker 1994)

is that a freshly struck stone, such as flint and obsidian, has been shown to be between 210 and 1050 times sharper (Sheets 1987, 231) which means the flesh will heal together more quickly and leave less scarring. Their use in delicate eye surgery is now advocated as the sharper edge does less damage to the tissue, the cleaner incision facilitates healing and the eye tends to move far less (due to less resistance to the blade), allowing for a more accurate incision (ibid). A freshly struck flint is also sterile, which means it can be used safely in a medical environment.

However, this is by no means a new practice as the bible tells us that "Joshua made flint knives and circumcised the Israelites" (Joshua 5:3). The human affair with flint seems set to continue.

7. Making Archaeological Interpretations From Lithics

Is trying to understand past human behaviour from the study of stone tools really an attempt to squeeze blood from stones? Archaeologists believe this not to be the case as insights into many aspects of prehistoric archaeology have been gained through the systematic study of stone tools. By analysing the variations in form, function, distribution, raw material type, manufacturing technology, contextual circumstances and other archaeological associations, archaeologists have drawn on this battery of investigative strategies to make inferences about the past.

The study of stone tools in archaeology has long been associated with the study of technology. Stone tools are made using prescribed flaking techniques to produce repetitious tool forms; this allows stone tools to be classified into types according to size, shape, function, age, flaking technology and stage in the *chaîne opératoire*. This classification of artefacts into related groups, or 'typologies' as they are known in archaeology, remains one of the fundamental skills of the prehistoric archaeologist (see Andrefsky 1998). In recent years, though, the need to understand stone tool material culture in relation to its social context of production, use and discard has also been established (see Edmonds 1995). In this latter approach, lithic implements are viewed not just as functional tools but also as material expressions of art, symbol, beliefs, identity, social status and so on. Rather than being regarded as merely passive objects utilised in mundane tasks, stone tools are viewed as also having the potential to participate in social reproduction through their contexts of production, use, exchange and discard. This has also led to the use of stone tools for examining aspects of cognitive human behaviour, particularly in Palaeolithic studies (e.g. Mellars and Stringer 1989).

Lithic Identification and Attribute Analysis

Lithic analysis typically includes measuring the length, width and thickness of an artefact as well as recording its weight (metrical analysis), in order to produce a series of statistics that describe any given piece. The length-width ratio, for example, gives an indication of how long a flake is in relation to its width. Flakes with a length-width ratio of 2:1 or greater are usually assumed to be blades and if the ratio is less than 2:1 then they are thought to be flake tools; however, these proportions should be used only as a guide as blades can be more squat with a lower length-width ratio. If an assemblage is dominated by flakes with a length-width ratio of 2:1 or more it would be classified as belonging to a blade-based industry. However, blades do not necessarily have to be twice as long as they are wide as it is the intentional flaking of a linear detachment, often with parallel sides, that creates a blade form. Appendix 1 contains a list of the typical attributes to record when analysing a lithic assemblage.

The classification of flints can be hampered by the widespread plough damage that is common on lithic artefacts recovered from arable fields. Identification can be obscured by parts of the piece being missing or by edge damage appearing similar to intentional retouch, so it is important to be able to distinguish between breaks resulting from modern plough damage and intentional chipping (see Mallouf 1982). Useful explanations of how to get started in measuring, describing, analysing and classifying lithic artefacts can be found in Andrefsky (1998), Saville (1980) and also Watson (1968). Examples of the application of metrical analyses to inform archaeological interpretations include those by Pitts (1978), Pitts and Jacobi (1979), Burton (1980) and Myers (1987).

Functional Analysis

Identifying the function of stone tools is not simply an intuitive process. It is complicated by the fact that many stone tools may have been used for a number of purposes and even certain 'types' may have been used to perform a variety of tasks. Identifying a tool's function/s can be made difficult by the recycling of the piece for a different function at a later stage. Apart from occasions when artefacts are found still in their position of use, for example as arrowheads in a skeleton, the principal way in which the function of stone tools can be recognised is by experimental work, and to some extent by ethnographic analogy.

Experimental work has generally taken two forms. Firstly, there are those experiments that have sought to confirm a preconceived tool function, such as chopping down a tree with a stone axe head (Fig. 83), scraping the fat from a hide with a scraper (Fig. 84), and so on, to test whether such tasks could have been achieved using those particular types of tools. Secondly, there are macro-and micro-wear experiments which involve performing a variety of tasks using a given type, or types, of tool form and then analysing, either by eye or under a microscope, the distinctive wear patterns that are left after certain activities have been performed (e.g. Grace 1989). The three main types of wear traces are edge damage, polishes and striations. Wear pattern recognition relies on matching the wear patterns produced by known tasks, as a result of experimental work, with those observed on ancient stone tools. Scandinavian archaeologists have been particularly keen on replicating flesh penetration experiments, such as the point shooting exercises using animal carcasses by Fischer *et al* (1984), although others have carried out experimental flint knapping to answer questions regarding technological development (e.g. Callahan 1985; Crabtree 1968). A good starting point for studying experimental flint knapping is the book by Whittaker (1994) as well as Lord's booklet (1993) and the paper by Johnson (1978). Useful

83 - Chopping down a tree using a facsimile stone axe made from Langdale tuff as part of the experiment to 'reconstruct' a henge at the Maelmin Heritage Trail

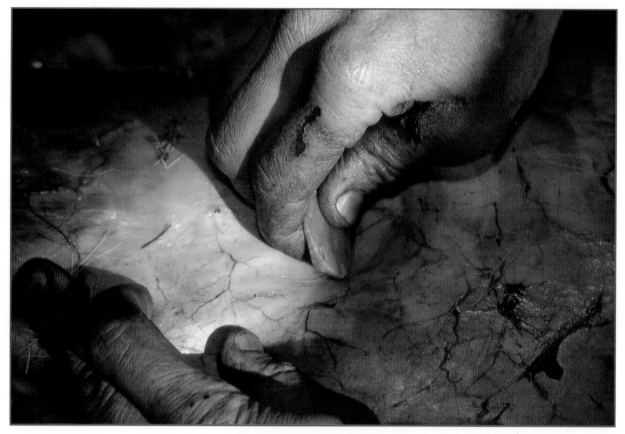

84 - Scraping the hide of a roe deer using a flint scraper

publications dealing with microwear analysis include those by Anderson (1980), Dumont (1988), Grace (1989) and Newcomer *et al* (1987). A new area of research that is in its infancy is the examination of residues on lithics. This type of analysis seeks to identify the biochemical signature of a residue and then equate this with the chemical profiles of known substances. In this way it is hoped that a more accurate indication of the use of a tool may be acquired. It is important that flints are not washed prior to examination if this analysis is to be carried out.

Spatial Analysis

Stone tools of particular kinds are often thought to be indicative of certain types of activities common to certain types of sites. For example, microliths are usually associated with kill sites and hunting camps whereas scrapers, borers and other processing tools, as well as some microliths, are usually associated with settlement sites. Bashed lumps and primary flakes, however, are most commonly found associated with raw material extraction sites (i.e. quarries). These generalisations are important, particularly to landscape archaeologists, who are concerned with trying to understand the changing pattern of human behaviour through time at the landscape scale. However, interpretation of surface lithic scatters can be problematic as it is not always clear whether stone tools have accumulated as a result of a single stay or repeat visits over a long period. The accretion of archaeological residues through time in the same place is known as a palimpsest and is an important consideration when attempting to understand and interpret stone tool distributions.

The primary method by which lithic artefacts are acquired and used to inform us about the distribution of human activities at the landscape scale is by fieldwalking. Fieldwalking consists of walking across ploughed fields in a systematic fashion, observing the exposed surface for stone tools and then recording the findspot of each piece as it is bagged. This allows prehistoric activities and their location to be identified. Although this method can be useful for identifying 'sites' it also allows patterns of land-use across the wider landscape to be understood. Consequently this fieldwork method is particularly informative for the study of mobile prehistoric groups, such as hunter-gatherers or pastoralists, as the method itself is directly compatible with the geographical scale at which such people lived out their existence. Fieldwalking studies have been undertaken across landscapes throughout the British Isles, but the key studies which have been conducted in north-east England are those in Weardale (Young 1987), County Durham (Haselgrove *et al* 1988), Tynedale (Tolan-Smith 1997) and the Milfield Basin (Waddington 1999a).

At the other end of the spatial scale, differentiation of activities on a specific site can sometimes be identified by accurately mapping and recording the distribution of particular lithic types. A good example of the differentiation of activity areas within a single site is that inferred by Smith (1992, 98-103) at Hengistbury Head. Here, on the basis of excavations by Mace, and later Campbell, he identifies certain areas of the site with bone and antler working, others with the preparation and repair of points (hunting gear) and others with stone tool working. Intra-site spatial analysis has also been employed by Grøn (1987; 1989; 1995) and Blankholm (1985; 1993) to identify the extent of possible structures at various sites and to examine questions relating to the social organization of space and its implications for social structure.

Production and Exchange

Scientific study of the provenance of rock types allows lithic implements to be matched with their geological source locations. In particular, instrumental neutron activation analysis (INAA) has been used to demonstrate that prehistoric groups occupying the Eckles site on the Great Plains of North America were prepared to travel distances of up to 450km in order to acquire the Chadron Formation chert from Flattop Bute rather than use other types of more locally available chert (Hoard *et al* 1992, 663). Electron microprobe analysis has also been used successfully to provenance chert and obsidian and other mineralogically homogeneous rocks (see Kempe and Templeman 1983). Indeed, it is now well known that Paleoindians travelled vast distances to obtain chert throughout the Americas (see Ellis and Lothrop 1989). In the British Isles the Council for British Archaeology's stone axe study has succeeded in the petrological identification of axe groups made from a wide variety of rock sources in northern and western Britain (Clough and Cummins 1979; 1988). This is of particular importance to archaeologists as it allows for the study of mobility patterns both in terms of the extent of annual rounds of itinerant groups (in the same way as the Early Mesolithic hunter-gatherers of the South Pennines, Chapter 5) as well as the direction and extent of exchange routes (as in the case of stone axe sources, Chapter 6). Other sources of information on the various scientific methods of lithic provenancing can be found in Andrefsky (1998) and Rapp and Hill (1998).

Once specific source areas have been identified, such as flint mines or stone-axe head quarries, archaeological excavations can provide information regarding the dates at which these sources were exploited, how resource extraction was organised, the manufacturing routines employed and the type of output produced (e.g. Barber *et al* 1999; Bradley and Edmonds 1993; Holgate 1991; Mercer 1981b; Saville 1995). However, not all flint sources come from a single deposit and few sources are visible in the landscape today so it is usually only the larger mining sites that can be recognised from surface observations and aerial photographs.

Social, Stylistic and Symbolic Interpretations

A recent trend in lithic studies is the application of theoretical approaches, widespread in other areas of prehistoric archaeology since the mid 1980s, to the analysis of stone tools. These new approaches recognise the importance of material culture in reflecting, and perhaps bringing about, social change (e.g. Edmonds 1995). For example, the association between exotic lithic artefacts, such as highly finished barbed and tanged arrowheads, polished stone axes, chisels, maceheads and so on, and high status burials, where they appear as grave goods, has long been recognised. It is now widely accepted that such elaborate and often non-utilitarian artefacts served as prestige objects symbolising the power and status of the person with whom they were associated.

Distinctive changes in technology have been identified as reflecting changes in the social ordering of society. For example, Gero (1989) has proposed that the change from flaked to ground points reflected not just a change in subsistence strategies, but also a higher investment of labour, greater social control as reflected by the standardisation of such tool forms, and the restriction of knowledge pertaining to new production techniques. Such interpretations are difficult to validate but they can bring into focus a range of useful insights into the way societies may have organised and reproduced themselves through time and thus broaden our appreciation of possible patterns of social behaviour.

Finely-made stone tools, such as polished maceheads, the more exquisite arrowheads, and daggers associated with individual burials are perhaps indicative of the emergence of an overt elite within society and, therefore, a more explicit social hierarchy. This provides a further illustration of how lithic objects may have been entwined in webs of social and political relations. As Edmonds has recently stated, "tools may not determine the character of society, but they are nonetheless caught up in the process by which the social order is continually brought into being" (1995, 14).

The recognition of differences in 'style' (i.e. distinctive appearance) has led some archaeologists to define distinct cultural groups, such as the Mesolithic social groupings Jacobi recognised across Britain (Jacobi 1978 and 1979), the differentiation of Mesolithic groups between the Rhine and the Wesser (Arora 1973), and the recognition of stylistic groups in the Late Mesolithic of southern Scandinavia (Vang Peterson 1984) and across other areas of north-western Europe (Gendel 1984). Although stylistic traits may indeed reflect cultural distinctions, such approaches rely heavily on subjective criteria to differentiate styles and other explanations may account for some of the explicitly observed differences, such as chronological or functional differences. Either way such studies are important as they focus attention on notions of identity and ethnicity, which according to most ethnographic studies, is a key concern in hunter-gatherer and early farming societies.

In a different vein, a recent study by the author contrasted Earlier Neolithic symbolic forms with those of the Later Neolithic. This study considered stone arrowhead types as well as pottery forms and rock art and related them to their context of deployment (Waddington 1998, 45-49). The principal finding was that all these material artefacts, well known as symbolically charged objects, show a progression from curvilinear shapes echoing patterns observable in the natural world to angular geometric shapes more typical of patterns produced through human notions of geometry and balance, that is, patterns ultimately conceived in the human mind. This transition in the shape and decoration of powerful symbolic media, in addition to changes in their context of deployment, has been interpreted as reflecting an important ideological shift in the way people understood and related to the (natural) world around them. Such views can, and are, contested because it is virtually impossible to supply proofs of such interpretative models no matter how likely or not they seem to be. However, it is important to recognise such changes in the aesthetic qualities of stone tool traditions because, like art of all periods, it gives a direct, though tantalising and somewhat ambiguous, glance into the cerebral world of the people who produced them.

The most up to date and in-depth work on the social context and interpretation of lithic artefacts is the study by Edmonds (1995). This contains a wide-ranging discussion of the role played by lithic material in the social worlds of Neolithic and Bronze Age communities in Britain in addition to supplying sections on further reading.

Appendix 1

List of attributes used in the recording of a lithic assemblage.

Small Find Number
Context
Material (e.g. flint, chert, quartz, agate)
Colour
Geological Origin (e.g. nodular, glacial or beach flint)
Whether Patinated
Whether Broken
Whether Burnt
Whether recycled
Type General (e.g. microlith)

Type Specific (e.g. scalene triangle)
Stage in Reduction Sequence (e.g. primary, secondary, tertiary)
Period (e.g. Late Mesolithic)
Length
Width
Thickness
Weight
Notes

The information can be recorded directly on to a spreadsheet or data base providing a powerful analytical tool that can be used to identify patterns in the data. In addition, graphs and charts can also be easily produced from this data in order to present results in a clear and comprehensible way in subsequent reports. When recording chipped stone assemblages in this way it is general practice not to record length, width, thickness and weight if a piece is broken as it only produces erroneous data; instead only whole pieces are measured for this information. Similarly, if a piece is completely patinated the colour is not recorded as the presence of the patina prevents accurate assessment of the actual colour of the flint.

Appendix 2

Lithic Illustration

The illustration of flint artefacts requires a thorough understanding of how flints have been struck and how such characteristics are then portrayed using appropriate conventions. The key manuals that help unlock the door to lithic illustration are those by Martingell and Saville (1988), Addington (1986) and the more general work by Griffiths *et al* (1990). A number of universities provide classes within Continuing Education Departments in archaeological illustration, while membership of the Association of Archaeological Illustrators (address given in the Further Information section) brings the benefits of seminars, conferences, publications and the opportunity to seek advice from professional illustrators.

Glossary of Terms

Abrupt Retouch A term used to refer to the rechipping of a prepared flake or blade by creating steep detachment scars with an angle of between 45 and 90 degrees from the striking platform.

Blade An intentionally produced linear flake, usually at least twice as long as it is broad, with the long sides often parallel.

Backed Blade/Bladelet A blade or bladelet that has been blunted by retouch down one side.

Biface A tool that has been retouched (usually invasively) on both its surfaces, such as a Palaeolithic hand axe. The manufacturing of a tool with retouch over both sides is termed bi-facial working.

Bipolar Flaking A technique that results in flakes being removed from opposed ends of a core or nodule. It is achieved by resting the core on an anvil stone and then striking with a hammer stone. This removes a flake and at the same time a countershock is produced by the hard surface on which the core was placed. The countershock causes another flake to be removed from this end of the core. Sometimes referred to as 'scalar flaking' this technique is useful for flaking small pebbles, although it often results in crushed platforms and reduces control over the shape of the flakes. It is most common in assemblages from northern and western Britain where access to large flint nodules is limited.

Bulb of Percussion This term refers to the smooth, raised, rounded hump on the ventral surface of a flake situated immediately below the striking platform. It is created by the impact of the hammer blow. Generally, the harder the hammer, and/or greater the force, the larger the bulb. The concavity caused on the core or nodule by the removal of the bulb is sometimes referred to as the negative bulb.

Burin A burin is the name given to a chisel-like implement made from a blade or flake that has been modified by the removal of a splinter. This involves the removal of a sliver of flint from either the long edge or either end of the blank. The splinter can be referred to as a burin spall. Burin spalls are usually a narrow sliver of flint with a triangular or trapezoidal cross-section.

Chaîne Opératoire See 'reduction sequence'

Chip A chip is a small irregular piece of stone (usually less than 5mm in length) that has been removed during the flaking process. Chips are waste products not usually intended for use or modification into tools and are often referred to as debitage. Particular forms of chip can be diagnostic of particular processes.

Composite Tool This is an implement which combines two or more tool group types on the one piece. This may include artefacts such as a burin with an end scraper or a core that has also been used as a scraper.

Conchoidal Fracture Rock types with either a very fine grain or regular crystalline structure fracture in a regular and predictable way when they are struck. Conchoidal means 'shell-like' with a smooth curved surface. In the case of flint, it flakes conchoidally so that pieces of the nodule's shell detach in layers, the thickness and shape of which can be controlled. Removals frequently have a slightly crescentic profile.

Core A (usually) prepared block of raw material from which flakes and blades are removed. Cores are classified into different types depending on the knapping technique employed, such as single platform cores, opposed platform cores, multi-platform cores, bi-polar cores, pyramidal cores, Levallois cores and so on. Such core types typically characterise the blade-based technologies of the Upper Palaeolithic, Mesolithic and Neolithic; core types of the Bronze Age are less regular and are not generally classified into specific types.

Core Rejuvenation A technique that allows the working of a core to be extended by correcting irregularities in the core's form. This may include creating a new platform, removing irregularities such as crushed areas of a platform or removing the entire striking platform by a lateral blow to create a fresh platform.

Core Tablet The flake removed across a worn or damaged platform to create a new platform for further working.

Cortex The outer surface, or skin, of a rock which forms as a result of water loss and chemical action. There is considerable variation in the types and degree to which different rocks acquire a cortex. The cortex on chalk flint is often thick, white and chalky, the cortex on glacial or gravel flint is often thin and abraded, while beach flint usually has a smooth, thick, encrusted cortex. The non-chalk sources of flint are from 'derived' deposits and can be of various colours. Therefore, the character of the cortex on artefacts can be used as a guide to the contextual origin of the raw material.

Cresting This term applies to the preparation of a core for the removal of blades or bladelets involving the creation of a longitudinal ridge to guide the first removal, with the result that parallel ridges are set up for further removals.

Debitage Derived from the French term meaning the process of stone tool production by flaking. However, it is more commonly used to refer to all categories of struck waste material, irrespective of size, produced during the flaking process. Small material, just a few millimetres in size, is sometimes referred to as microdebitage.

Denticulate This is a tool with at least three consecutive notches along one edge that form a series of teeth.

Distal End The end of a flake or blade opposite the struck end.

Dorsal Surface The outer or upper side of a flake/blade which carries the scars and ridges of previous removals. If it is a primary flake chipped off a nodule the dorsal surface will carry the cortex. The dorsal surface can provide information as to the flaking techniques practised as it often shows clear flake or blade scar removals.

Flake A generic term for any piece of stone that has been chipped from another piece of stone. Flakes occur in a vast array of forms, though they are usually more irregular than blades. The shape of a flake may be indicative of particular flaking traditions/techniques. Flakes can be subsequently modified into tools while others may be utilised without recourse to modification. The latter type are described as 'utilised flakes'.

Flintknapping The process of making stone tools by the flaking process.

Hammer Tool used to strike a stone in order to detach a flake. Hammers vary in size, hardness and material as this affects the type of blow that is delivered. Hard hammers are usually made of stone, such as quartzite or granite, while soft hammers include those made from wood, antler and softer stones, such as limestone. Hammers are sometimes referred to as 'percussors'.

Hand Axe A large knapped stone designed to be held in the hand and used in a pounding motion. Sometimes these tools are referred to as choppers. Hand axes date to the early and middle Palaeolithic periods and were used by early types of humans. They are not to be confused with ground and polished stone axe-heads.

Holocene Sometimes referred to as the Flandrian, this is the geological name for the inter-glacial period in which we now live.

Invasive Retouch The shaping of a flake or blade by the removal of slivers of flint at a very shallow angle to the edge (see also Fig. 19).

Levallois Flake This is the term given to a specific type of flake usually associated with Middle Palaeolithic flintworking. It is characterised by overlapping flake removal scars struck from opposite edges on its dorsal side and a smooth surface on its ventral side. Sometimes these flakes are referred to as tortoise flakes because of the shell-like pattern created by the scars on the dorsal surface. See also Fig. 18 and page 22.

Microburin A microburin is a waste piece from microlith manufacture. It is made by detaching usually the proximal (or 'bulbar') end of the blade (see Fig. 39) by notching, and then snapping, with the other end of the piece being further modified to produce a microlith. Microburins are generally the waste from microlith production although they are themselves sometimes utilised and/or occasionally retouched.

Microlith A small stone tool made by blunting the edges of tiny blades often made to specific forms. In Britain they are divided into geometric (e.g. scalene triangles, isosceles triangles, trapezes, rhomboids, crescents, backed blades, needle points and rods) and non-geometric forms (e.g. obliquely blunted points, backed points). The geometric forms are typical of the Late Mesolithic period while the non-geometric forms are associated with the Early Mesolithic. In addition the later geometric forms tend to be made on smaller narrow blade blanks while the earlier microliths tend to be made on larger and wider blade blanks. Used for a variety of purposes though most commonly used as armatures (barbs) in hunting weapons. These forms are the hallmark of the Mesolithic period.

Notched Tool An implement with a deep concavity on one edge produced either by a single blow, a series of small retouch removals or a pressure flake removal.

Nodule An unchipped lump of stone.

Obliquely blunted/truncated A feature on some blades and microliths whereby a snapped bladelet has had microlithic retouch across the snap running obliquely across the piece.

Patination More commonly referred to as recortication or cortication, this is the name given to the early stage in the re-formation of cortex on the surface of chipped stone tools. The process of patina formation remains poorly understood although it is a product of chemical action affected by the presence of water, weathering and soil conditions over time. As the timespan involved in cortex formation is considerable, the presence of patinas on stone tools is sometimes used as a proxy (though not definitive) indication of considerable age.

Percussion Flaking The flaking of a stone involving the direct use of a hammer (percussor) to detach flakes.

Platform The surface of a core or nodule that is struck to remove flakes or blades during the knapping process. It is sometimes called the striking platform. Although any suitable surface can be used, specially prepared flat platform surfaces are common. This allows the angle at the platform edge to be more carefully maintained as it is the angle at which a core is hit that determines the shape of the detached piece. Cores or nodules may have more than one platform.

Pressure Flaking This is a type of direct flaking which involves placing a pointed tool (usually of antler or bone) onto the edge of the piece being worked and then increasing the pressure on the tool until a flake is removed. This flaking strategy is frequently used in the latter stages of tool production, often to produce fine, thin and accurate removals.

Proximal End The end of the flake or blade at which the removal blow was struck. It is the end that contains the butt and the bulb of percussion and is therefore sometimes referred to as the 'bulbar' end.

Reduction Sequence This term refers to the series of stages that are followed when creating stone tools. The main stages of flaking a flint artefact run through nodule - primary flaking - secondary flaking - tertiary product (tool). Related to this term is the 'Chaîne Opératoire' which translates as the 'operational sequence'. This latter term has a wider significance as it refers to the entire sequence of stone tool production from the acquisition of the raw material through to the final discard of a tool.

Retouch The intentional modification of a flake or blade in order to shape it and prepare it for use. This may include sharpening an edge, blunting an edge or thinning a flake or blade.

Shouldered Points This is the name given to points commonly found on Late Palaeolithic sites. They include a shoulder, usually towards the pointed end of the piece, formed by retouch and frequently have oblique truncation at the opposite end.

Test Piece (or Bashed Lump) A nodule that has had a flake or two chipped off it, usually to find out the flaking quality of the nodule.

Ventral Surface The surface of the flake or blade which originally faced into the nodule/core. It is the smooth inner surface that occasionally has ripples caused by the shock of the hammer blow and the surface with the bulb of percussion.

Further Information

Societies

Lithic Studies Society: founded in 1979, it produces publications, organises conferences, seminars and trips and is a forum for discussion. Membership details can be obtained from: The Membership Secretary, Lithic Studies Society, c/o The British Museum, Quaternary Section, Franks House, 38-46 Orsman Road, London, N1 5QJ. The society also produces an annual journal, *Lithics*, which all members receive free of charge. Website: www.britarch.ac.uk/lithics/

Association of Archaeological Illustrators and Surveyors: for those wishing to further an interest in the illustration of lithic artefacts, the society arranges conferences and produces a range of useful publications. Membership details can be obtained from: AAI&S, c/o Department of History and Archaeology, University of Exeter, Queen's Building, Queen's Drive, Exeter, Devon, EX4 4QH.

Courses in the North-East

Information on adult education courses available to the general public covering various aspects of Stone Age archaeology in north-east England can be obtained from: The Centre for Lifelong Learning, King George VI Building, University of Newcastle upon Tyne, NE1 7RU.

Museums which hold lithic collections in the north-east of England include:

The Museum of Antiquities, The Quadrangle, University of Newcastle, NE1 7RU (0191 2227849).

Museum of Antiquities, Alnwick Castle, Estates Office, Northumberland, NE66 1NQ (01665 510777 ext 190).

The Bowes Museum, Barnard Castle, County Durham, DL12 8NP (01833 690606).

The Old Fulling Mill Museum, The Banks, Durham, DH1 3EB (0191 3743623).

Sunderland Museum, Borough Road, Sunderland, SR1 1PR (0191 553 2323).

Weardale Museum, c/o The Secretary, 7 Windyside, Westgate, Weardale, Co. Durham. (01388 537417).

World Wide Web Sites

The Stone Age Reference Collection: www.hf.uio.no/iakk/roger/lithic/sarc.html
Knappers Anonymous: www.geocities.com/knappersanonymous
The Early Materials Forum: www.ucl.ac.uk/emf/
The Lithics Site: http://wings.buffalo.edu/anthropology/lithics/index2.html
The Howick Mesolithic Site: www.ncl.ac.uk/howick
The Journal of Lithic Technology: www.cas.utulsa.edu/anthropology/lithictechnology

Gazetteer of Lithic Collections in the Museum of Antiquities, Newcastle upon Tyne

The Museum of Antiquities contains an extensive collection of flint assemblages, mostly from the north-east but with some material from further afield. Much of the material is the result of surface collection, usually from fields, and includes the collections of Francis Buckley, William Cocks, Frank Dodds, Tom Heyes and Joan Weyman amongst others. The largest single assemblage, however, is from the stratified deposits of a Mesolithic settlement site recently excavated by the author at Howick.

A wide variety of material is represented in the collection and includes flint, chert, quartz and agate artefacts. In general the north-east lithics tend to be small in size, evidently reflecting the small size of locally available raw materials such as the cherts, agates, beach and glacial flint. Most of the Mesolithic material is made from local flint while Neolithic and Bronze Age pieces are more frequently made from imported nodular flint. A common type of local flint that can be recognised is a speckled red-brown flint common in Northumberland coastal assemblages. There is also a ginger coloured flint and an orange flint found in coastal collections. Probably the most common material consists of varieties of light grey speckled flint, some of which can be found locally in boulder clay and as beach pebbles, but much of the material may have originated in the boulder clays of north-east Yorkshire.

Very few of the lithics contained in the Museum's collection come from dated contexts, although there is a considerable amount of material from *in situ* deposits that have datable associations, such as beakers, food vessel urns and so forth. Although there is an increasing number of Stone Age sites now being radiocarbon dated in the north-east, there remains only limited chronological control on the lithic sequences from this region. Consequently the overall classificatory schemes referred to in this text relate to dated material from elsewhere in the country, drawing on locally dated comparanda when available.

This gazetteer describes the collections of chipped stone and flint tools kept by the Museum of Antiquities. It does not include the stone axe heads, as these merit a publication in their own right, but flint axes have been included. The gazetteer is organized first by county (Northumberland, County Durham, Cleveland, Tyne and Wear, Yorkshire and Miscellaneous) with entries then ordered by place in alphabetical order. For each entry a National Grid reference is given, when this is known, together with the Museum's Catalogue Number, the donor and details of any published references. For each entry there is a brief summary of the assemblage with indication of any dating when possible.

Although the extensive lithic collections held by the Museum have generally received little attention by researchers there are some important additional notes accompanying some of the collections. The Cocks collection is notable in this respect as most of the finished tools have been drawn and have accompanying descriptions in a useful archive that also includes a database of all the material from the various sites, together with the box number and a copy of Cocks' original notebook. Most of the

Cocks material is from the lower Tyne valley in the vicinity of Ryton, Crawcrook and Claravale and is included in this gazetteer under the entry for Ryton.

The largest collection is that of the late Joan Weyman who was a leading authority on north-east English stone tools for many years. Dr. Weyman was an avid field walker during the 1970's and 1980's and discovered some outstanding sites around Northumberland including important locations in the Tyne Valley (e.g. High Warden, Gallowhill Farm, Low Shilford, Peepy Farm and Dewley Hill amongst others) and the Milfield Basin (particularly around Miket's site at Thirlings). She also made an important collection of flint material from the Yorkshire Wolds, which is held in the Museum of Antiquities. This includes many hundreds of flints recovered during fieldwalking and for which there is good locational information. Accompanying Dr. Weyman's collections are useful text archives that include grid references as well as drawings, descriptions and important interpretive notes.

The other large collection that requires special mention is that of Francis Buckley who collected predominantly on coastal sites in the north of Northumberland during the 1920's and 1930's and discovered important locations of Stone Age activity in a swathe of land running from Budle Bay in the north to Craster in the south. Particular concentrations of material were obtained from sites at Budle Bay, Bamburgh and Spindlestone. Some of these sites were published in local journals at the time and the references are provided under the appropriate site entries in the gazetteer.

ABBREVIATIONS

AA   *Archaeologia Aeliana*
AJ   *Archaeological Journal*
CBA   *Council for British Archaeology*
NA   *Northern Archaeology*
PPS   *Proceedings of the Prehistoric Society*
PSAN   *Proceedings of the Society of Antiquaries of Newcastle upon Tyne*

For some finds/assemblages a full six or eight figure National Grid reference can be cited but for other entries, where there is little locational information, no grid reference is given. The abbreviation Cat. No. is an abbreviation for the Museum of Antiquities catalogue number.

NORTHUMBERLAND

Acklington

Acklington Aerodrome
Cat. No. 1945.2
Donor: A.R. Robson
A broken polished flint axe, dark grey at edge shading to yellow-brown at butt. Neolithic. Found by an airman at the aerodrome.

Acomb

NY 9332 0037
Cat. No. 1996.4.2
Bequest: Dr. J. Weyman
A single light grey flint flake.

Akeld

NT 951 300
Cat. No. 1996.8
Bequest: Dr. J. Weyman
A single, tiny, light grey broken flint bladelet. A separately bagged collection of 4 agate chips, 1 light grey broken flint bladelet, 1 retouched chert flake and 1 quartz chip. Another bag containing two red agate chips.

Allendale

Near Chimneys, Allendale Town
NY 814 539
Cat. No. 1984.2
Donor: K.A. Bennett
A collection of 47 flints found whilst fieldwalking near the chimneys. Flints are of different types and date. One very fine barbed and tanged arrowhead and another with a broken tang. There are many blade pieces including edge-trimmed blades indicative of Mesolithic or Neolithic activity. There is also a broken blade with sharpened edge made of good quality nodular flint that probably served as a knife, together with another broken knife-type implement made of light grey speckled flint. Mesolithic-Bronze Age.

Allendale Smeltmills
Cat. No. 1994.8
Donor: Tyne and Wear Museums
3 flint flakes and a fragment of slag. Two of the flints are patinated but all three are of a light grey speckled variety.

Allendale
NY 819 539
Cat. No. 1996.5.1
Bequest: Dr. J. Weyman
A single grey flint broken scraper.

Allendale
NY 800 521
Cat. No. 1996.5.1
Bequest: Dr. J. Weyman
A single medium grey flint blade.

Allendale
NY 810 535
Cat. No. 1996.5.1
Bequest: Dr. J. Weyman
A single light grey speckled flake.

Alnham

High Knowes, Alnham
NT 971 125
Cat. No. 1979.21.A
Donor: Prof. G. Jobey
Refs: *AA* 4th ser. 44 (1966): 5-48
Collection of 17 flint and chert artefacts found during Jobey's excavations at High Knowes, Alnham. Pieces include a barbed and tanged arrowhead, scrapers, blades and flakes. Neolithic-Early Bronze Age.

Alnmouth

Alnmouth Area
Cat. No. 1999.18
Donor: Northampton Museum (previous accession number: 9217.1-2)
2 flints including one broken dark grey flint with blade removal scars on dorsal side and one patinated medium grey blade segment with steep retouch along one edge and light marginal retouch on the opposite edge.

Alnwick

1 mile west of Alnwick
Cat. No. 1939.13
Donor: A.R. Robson
Refs: *PSAN* 4th ser. 9 (1940): 97
A Neolithic leaf-shaped flint arrowhead, or possible spear tip, made from an orange-brown mottled flint recovered from somewhere 1 mile west of Alnwick. Neolithic.

Amble

Amble
Cat. No. 1923.3
Donor: Mr. E. Hunter
Refs: *PSAN* 4th ser. 1 (1925): 8
A very fine flint spear point made from a dark grey flint that came from an inhumation burial, which contained a broken 'urn'. Late Neolithic-Early Bronze Age.

Apperley Dene

Castle Hill summit, 1.5km NW of Whittonstall
NZ 056 581
Cat. No. 1979.48
Donor: Dr. K. Greene
Refs: *AA* 5th ser. 6 (1978): 57-58
Collection of 15 lithics recovered during archaeological excavations of the Apperley Dene Roman site. Most of the 14 flint pieces showed signs of use. Notable pieces include a burin, leaf-arrowhead and core-trimming flake. Late Mesolithic-Early Neolithic. There is also a hollow scraper made from chert.

Bamburgh

Shada Crags
Cat. No. 1922.6
Donor: F. Buckley
Refs: *PSAN* 3rd ser. 10 (1923): 271
             PSAN 4th ser. 3 (1929): 92
A single barbed and tanged flint arrowhead and single flake of the same material from Shada Crags, Bamburgh, and another two from an area around Luckermoorhouse. Microliths from Bamburgh and Craster. Mesolithic-Early Bronze Age.

Bamburgh-Craster coastline
Cat. No. 1922.24
Donor: F. Buckley
A fine collection of 56 card-mounted flints including microliths (comprising geometric forms, crescents, backed blades and points), a variety of scrapers, a knife, blades and some retouched flakes. Late Mesolithic.

Bamburgh District
Cat. No. 1935.16-18
Donor: F. Buckley
Lithic assemblage comprising 12 pieces resulting from surface collection. The assemblage consists mostly of flint pieces, one of which is a retouched broken blade segment with the rest mostly flakes and debitage. Mesolithic.

Bardon Mill

NY 7735 6467
Cat. No. 1996.4.2
Bequest: Dr. J. Weyman
A patinated flake and a dark grey utilised blade.

Bearl Farm

Tyne Valley
NZ 0535 6370
Cat. No. 1996.4.2
Bequest: Dr. J. Weyman
A single light grey flint flake.

Bellingham

The Sneep, Bellingham
Cat. No. 1910.15
Bequest: Mr. J.R.D. Lynn
Refs: *PSAN* 3rd ser. 4 (1910): 286
             AA 2nd ser. 15 (1892): 49-53
A cist containing an inhumation found on the banks of the Tarset Burn at The Sneep contained a beaker which lay on its side behind the shoulder of a skeleton with 7 roughly worked flints and 2 flint nodules positioned immediately outside the lip of the vessel. The flints may, therefore, have originally been placed inside the pot.

Belling Law

Belling Law Enclosure
NY 686 882
Cat. No. 1979.27
Donor: Prof. G. Jobey
Refs: *AA* 5th ser. 5 (1977): 29
Flint assemblage recovered during Jobey's excavations of the Belling Law Iron-Age settlement. Total of 27 lithics made from chert and flint including 4 scrapers of Late Neolithic-Early Bronze Age date. Most of the flints are from the surface of the underlying clay in the north and west parts of the site with only 5 stratified beneath the counterscarp bank and core of the inner wall.

Bellshiel

Bellshiel Long Cairn
NT 813 011
Cat. No. 1935.26-28
Donor: Miss. N. Newbiggin
Refs: *AA* 4th ser. 13 (1936): 293-309
During excavations on the Bellshiel Law long cairn, situated in the Otterburn Army range, 2 pieces of burnt flint were recovered. Neolithic.

Bellshiel Round Cairn
NT 813 010
Cat. No. 1935.30
Donor: Miss. N. Newbiggin
Refs: *PSAN* 4th ser. 7 (1937): 121-2
A single light grey flint thumbnail scraper recovered during excavations on a round cairn. Early Bronze Age.

Bewick

NU 054 228
Cat. No. 1996.4.1
Bequest: Dr. J. Weyman
A collection of 8 light grey flints including blades, flakes and a core.

Bikerton

NU 0003 0037
Cat. No. 1996.4.1
Bequest: Dr. J. Weyman
A single patinated flint flake.

Biddlestone Edge

NT 970 070
Cat. No. 1996.4.1
Bequest: Dr. J. Weyman
A single grey flint bladelet.

Birtley

Birtley Churchyard
NY 878 780
Cat. No. 1925.14.1
Donor: Ms. Hall
Refs: *PSAN* 4th ser. 2 (1927): 90
A barbed and tanged flint arrowhead found 5' 6" below the ground surface in the foundations of the vestry tower of Birtley Church (North Tyne). Late Neolithic-Early Bronze Age date.

Black Callerton

NZ 1774 7115
Cat. No. 1996.5.1
Bequest: Dr. J. Weyman
A single fawn coloured flint scraper.

Bolam Lake

Sandyford Quarry Field
NZ 075 817
Cat. No. 2002.16
Donor: Clive Waddington and John Davies
Refs: *NA* 15/16 (1998): 45-50
AA 5th ser. 30 (2002): 1-47.

A total of 37 lithics from the excavation of an Early Neolithic settlement site. It is a cohesive assemblage resulting from a blade-based manufacturing tradition and, assuming it is all contemporary with the radiocarbon dates from the site, dates the material to *c.*3700BC (Cal.). The assemblage includes a number of broken blades and flakes together with a scraper, leaf-shaped arrowhead, core and various retouched flakes and blades. Most of the material is grey flint, though a broken Group VI stone axe head and a flake, possibly from the same axe, were also found in one of the pits. The lithic assemblage was fully published in the article in *Archaeologia Aeliana* (see above).

Bothal

NZ 2300 8530
Cat. No. 1996.5.1
Bequest: Dr. J. Weyman
A burnt flint core and a red-brown broken flake.

Bothal
NZ2385 8630
Cat. No. 1996.5.1
Bequest: Dr. J. Weyman
A collection of two light grey flint flakes and a patinated flint flake.

Bothal
NZ 2325 8650
Cat. No. 1996.5.1
Bequest: Dr. J. Weyman
A light grey and a dark grey flake made from flint.

Bowden Doors

Bowden Doors
NU 070 327
Cat. No. 1998.5
Donor: Northumbria Mountaineering Club
Ref: *AA* 5th ser. 27 (1999): 173-4.
A total of 16 flints found by climbers over a number of years. The collection includes an opposed platform core, broken scraper, snapped pointed blade and retouched flake in addition to unmodified flakes and blades. Material includes light grey, orange, white and khaki flint together with two burnt pieces. Mesolithic.

Colourheugh Crag
NU 07 32
Cat. No. 1998.4
Donor: Northumbria Mountaineering Club
Ref: AA 5th ser. 27 (1999): 173-4.
3 flints found by climbers including a small agate blade, a broken retouched blade tool and a utilised blade. Probably Mesolithic.

Breamish Valley

Breamish Valley
Field 1 NT9675 1627
Field 2 NT 9737 1625
Field 3 NT 9732 1605
Cat. Nos. 1997.23, 1997.24, 1997.25
Donor: RCHME, Newcastle Office
Finds collected during fieldwalking from 3 fields in the Upper Breamish Valley. They include 1 broken dark-grey flint flake, possibly of nodular origin. Undiagnostic.

Brockdam

Brockdam
Cat. No. 1979.49
Donor: S. Beckensall
Assemblage of 11 flints from excavations by donor at Brockdam. Includes a blade core, flakes and a pointed blade tool. Late Mesolithic-Early Neolithic.

Budle

Budle-Craster
Cat. No. 1922.27
Donor: F. Buckley
Assemblage of 181 small flint chips recovered during field collection along the coast between Budle and Craster. Mostly light and medium grey flint. Many blade forms, blade waste and blade scars evident, which suggests a Late Mesolithic date. Very little patinated material and a few cores.

Budle Bay
Cat. No. 1927.139
Donor: F. Buckley
Collection of 9 lithics found as surface finds from Alnmouth, Budle Bay, Ross Links and Luckermoorhouse. The collection includes 5 tiny scrapers with steep retouch, including one made from chert, two flakes, a barbed and tanged arrowhead with broken tip and barbs, and a piece of sandstone. Mesolithic-Bronze Age.

Budle Bay
Cat. No. 1933.32-34
Donor: F. Buckley
3 lithics: 2 from Budle Crags and one from Bamburgh. The two

Budle pieces are flakes, one of which is heavily burnt, the other being edge-trimmed. The Bamburgh piece is a retouched chert tool, possibly a scraper, with abrupt retouch. Probably Mesolithic.

Budle Crags
Cat. No. 1922.7.1-3
Donor: F. Buckley
Refs: PSAN 3rd ser. 10 (1923): 271
2 flint cores and a quartz pebble hammer stone found during surface collection. Both cores have narrow bladelet scars suggesting production of blanks for microliths. Later Mesolithic.

Budle Crags
Cat. No. 1922.26
Donor: F. Buckley
Refs: PSAN 3rd ser. 10 (1923): 271
Assemblage of 294 small flint chips found during surface collection. Includes light grey speckled flint together with local pebble flint and occasional orange-grey glacial flint and darker grey flint. Some of the flints are recycled. Overall the flaking scars and flake shapes suggest a generally Late Mesolithic date for this material.

Budle
NU 1335
Cat.No. 1935.31
Donor: A.R.Robson
Ref: PSAN 4th series, 7, 122
Axehead of light brown flint, darker at the edges. Polished at the cutting edge but roughly chipped on the other edges and both surfaces.

Bywell

NZ 034 621
Cat. Nos. 1982.3, 1982.12, 1982.16, 1982.20
Donor: Trustees of the Bywell Estate.
A large collection of 310 flints found during laying of gas pipeline. An important collection of flints from various fields. It includes a lot of flakes and waste material but also a fine plano-convex knife, cores and scrapers. A variety of flint types are represented including light grey speckled, red-brown, orange-grey and occasional dark grey flint. Forms indicate dates ranging from Mesolithic through to Early Bronze Age. This is an important assemblage that requires further attention.

Peepy Farm, Bywell
Bequest: Dr. J. Weyman
Cat. No. 1996.2.1

NZ 043 626	7 flints, 1 flint nodule, 1 stone
NZ 038 634	10 flints
NZ 044 633	7 flints
NZ 043 634	10 flints, 1 glass fragment
NZ 039 630	3 flints

Cat. No. 1996.2.2

NZ 029 633	200 flints, 5 quartz pieces
NZ 028 634	44 flints, 1 quartz
NZ 031 636	2 flints, 1 quartz
NZ 033 634	2 flints
NZ 035 634	1 quartz
NZ 027 634	2 flints
NZ 031 629	8 flints
NZ 030 628	6 flints
NZ 029 629	5 flints
NZ 027 635	23 flints

Cat. No. 1996.2.3

NZ 041 620	73 flints, 2 quartz
NZ 032 619	1 flint
NZ 035 620	11 flints, 4 quartz, 1 glass fragment
NZ 034 620	9 flints
NZ 035 622	37 flints
NZ 037 623	10 flints
NZ 038 619	12 flints

Fieldwalking over 16 fields recovered a total of 446 lithics in addition to waste flints from Eastern Fields, Riverside Fields and Stoneyverge Fields. This is an important collection of lithic material which comprises mostly flint but also quartz pieces. There is a wide variety of material including red, red-brown, orange-grey, ginger, light grey and dark grey flint. Much of it is waste material though the collection includes cores, blades, flakes, scrapers and a number of microliths of mostly narrow blade geometric forms. There is an interesting, recycled, heavily patinated blade that may have been originally chipped during the Upper Palaeolithic. This relatively well-recorded collection merits a full assessment, particularly in relation to characterizing North-Eastern Late Mesolithic sites from surface lithic scatters. Overall Late Mesolithic date for this assemblage.

Carrawburgh

Carrawburgh Roman Fort
NY 859 711
Cat. No. 1970.14
Donor: Mr. R. du Cane
Refs: AA 4th ser. 50 (1972): 118
2 flints were found during excavations at Carrawburgh Fort on Hadrian's Wall. They include a barbed and tanged arrowhead (Late Neolithic-Early Bronze Age) and a retouched parallel-sided flint blade (Probably Late Mesolithic-Early Neolithic).

Charlton Mires

Charlton Mires
Cat. No. 1975.17
Donor: Mr. R. Robson
2 large utilized flint flakes found together in peat at about 5 feet depth during ditch deepening 100yds, west of 'Patterson's Cottage' near Charlton Mires. Possibly Late Neolithic-Early Bronze Age.

Chathill

'Stoney Fads' Field, Newsteads Farm
Cat. No. 1975.2
Donor: Mr. J. Shiels
Single broken barbed and tanged flint arrowhead made from a light grey flint. Late Neolithic-Early Bronze Age.

Chatton Moor

Stell Knowe
NU 114 250
Cat. No. 1978.17
Donor: Forestry Commission
A single flint knife recovered from the ploughed out remains of a Bronze Age cairn excavated by the Field Research Group of the Society of Antiquaries of Newcastle upon Tyne in 1975.

Foumart Knowe
NU 107 254
Cat. Nos. 1973.7a, 1973.7b
Donor: T. Smith
An assemblage of 30 flints and 2 fragments of ground and polished stone axe-heads found during forestry planting undertaken in spring 1973. The flint assemblage includes a steeply retouched Late Mesolithic scraper made from light grey speckled flint, a dark grey flint scraper, blades and flakes. There are also flakes of orange, red-brown, white and yellow flint. Late Mesolithic-Neolithic.

Chatton Sandyford Moor

Cairnfield
NU 100 266
Cat. No. 1979.36
Donor: Prof. G. Jobey
Refs: AA 4th ser. 46 (1968): 27-9
A total of 4 flint scrapers and 2 retouched pointed blade tools that have scraper affinities, recovered during Jobey's excavations of Bronze Age cairns on Chatton Sandyford Moor, Northumberland. Early Bronze Age.

Forestry south-east of Hangwell Law
NU 126 242
Cat. No. 1979.67
Donor: T. Heyes
A total of 4 lithics collected as surface finds from forestry area. Includes one piece of chipped agate, one piece of chipped chert and 2 pieces of poor quality flint. Undiagnostic.

Cheviots

No further provenance known
Cat. No. 1947.7
Donor: J.D. Cowen
A dark grey translucent flint chipped to a symmetrical shape and further polished at the cutting edge on both faces. Bought in August 1938 from Mr. G.T. Lowes of Allendale who had it from cottagers from the Cheviot area.

Cheviot Hills
NT 29
Cat.No.1947.7
Donor: J.D.Cowen who bought it in August 1938 from G.T.Lowes of Allendale who had acquired it, without a history, from cottagers in the Cheviot area.
Ref: PSAN 4th ser. 11 (1951); 138-40
Long, narrow axe head of grey flint, polished at the cutting edge but the other edges and both surfaces are roughly chipped.

Chillingham

Chillingham
Cat. No. 1963.12
Donor: Mr. L.C. Levi
Bronze Age flint knife from a depth of 5-6 feet together with animal bones and rim of Roman jar.

Chollerford

Chollerford
Cat. No. 1956.367.A
A single Early Bronze Age flint from a cist discovered in 1886.

Coldwell

Coldwell Farm
NZ 956 763
Cat. No. 1996.4.4
Bequest: Dr. J. Weyman
A total of 18 flints collected by fieldwalking from various findspots. Mostly light and medium grey flint including blade cores, flakes, blades and a broken microlith. Mesolithic.

Fell House, Coldwell
NZ 9568 7639
Cat. No. 1996.4.4
Bequest: Dr. J. Weyman
A total of 3 flints collected by fieldwalking including 1 light grey scraper with abrupt retouch, 1 brown serrated blade and 1 burnt flake. Late Mesolithic-Early Neolithic.

Colwell Fell

NY 958 765
Cat. No. 1996.5.1
Bequest: Dr. J. Weyman
6 light grey and burnt flint flakes.

Colwell Fell
NY 961 747
Cat. No. 1996.5.1
Bequest: Dr. J. Weyman
A single medium grey broken flint flake.

Corbridge

Caistron field
NY 995 654
Cat. No. 1932.75
Donor: R.C. and W.P. Hedley
Refs: PSAN 4th ser. 1 (1925): 111
PSAN 4th ser. 5 (1932): 329
Assemblage of 100 flints from an area of a field called the 'Caistron' near Corbridge. The collection includes one retouched blade, a scraper and 3 retouched flakes with the rest predominantly waste with many pieces broken, probably as a result of plough damage. The flint is of two main types: light grey speckled flint and red-brown flint. There is one heavily patinated piece that is probably more ancient than the rest of the assemblage which is associated with a blade-based industry showing Mesolithic affinities.

High Barns near Corbridge
NZ 016 632
Cat. No. 1979.65
Donor: T. Heyes
Collection of 8 flints from High Barns. Light grey and dark grey flint. Apart from one bladelet scar suggesting Late Mesolithic-Early Neolithic date, undiagnostic.

Thornborough Scar, Corbridge
NZ 011 632
Cat. No. 1983.6
Donor: T. Gates
A single light grey flint found during fieldwalking. Undiagnostic except for a narrow bladelet scar on dorsal surface.

Corbridge
NZ 0110 6488
Cat. No. 1996.4.2
Bequest: Dr. J. Weyman
A single grey flint flake.

Corbridge
Caistron Field
NY 995 654
Cat. No. 1996.4.2
Bequest: Dr. J. Weyman
A collection of 31 flints mostly burnt or light grey. Includes cores, blades, flakes and is probably Mesolithic.

Corby's Crags

Corby's Crags
NU 127 102
Cat. No. 1989.22
Donor: Ms. Meg Shaw
Very fine barbed and tanged light grey flint arrowhead found by climber. Early Bronze Age.

Corchester

Corchester
Cat. No. 1935.23
Donor: Mr. H. Preston
A single flint core.

Craster

The Heughs
Cat. No. 1922.5.1-2
Donor: F. Buckley
Refs: *PSAN* 3rd ser. 10 (1923): 271
PSAN 4th ser. 13 (1929): 92
2 leaf-shaped arrowheads, one made from a pale grey flint and another made from a light brown flint. Surface finds of Early Neolithic date and one leaf-shaped arrowhead from the north side of Budle Bay on the flint and pathway sites at Ross Links.

Cresswell

Cresswell
NZ 283 942 and NZ 285 942
Cat. No. 1996.4.4
Bequest: Dr. J. Weyman
A total of 23 lithics collected by fieldwalking including 14 quartz pieces which include pebbles, cores and flakes.

Darras Hall

Cat. No. 1996.4.2
Bequest: Dr. J. Weyman
A single ginger flint flake and a blade-shaped piece of mudstone.

Debdon Moor

Debdon Moor
Cat. No. 1969.29
Donor: Lord Armstrong
Refs: *CBA North 3 News Bulletin*, Sept. 1971
A collection of 15 flint flakes together with a jet/shale ring and charcoal discovered during works on Debdon Moor East. One opposed platform core with bladelet removals, probably Late Mesolithic.

Dour Hill

Dour Hill, Redesdale
NT 792 021
Cat. No. 1933.2
Donor: Drs. Punshon and Miller
Refs: *PSAN* 4th ser. 6 (1935): 18, 40
AA 5th ser. (1998): 1-15
A mottled grey flint scraper found in a secondary cist burial inserted into the Dour Hill chambered cairn. Early Bronze Age.

Duddo

Duddo Stone Circle Field
NT 933 438
Cat. No. 1985.12
Donor: Mr. C. Holder
A single flint hollow scraper found approx. 50 yards east of Duddo stone circle. Neolithic.

Duddo Stone circle Field
NT 930 437
Cat. No. 1999.4
Donor: Dr. C. Waddington
A single parallel-sided blade of white flint found 10m west of stone circle in ploughed field. Late Mesolithic-Neolithic.

Dunstanburgh

Dunstanburgh
Cat. No. 1956.165.1-2.A
A late Mesolithic microlith from Scrog Hill near Dunstanburgh Castle. Mesolithic.

Eachwick

NZ 112 693
Cat. No. 1996.4.2
Bequest: Dr. J. Weyman
A single light grey flint flake.

Edlingham

Edlingham forestry area
Cat. No. 1979.58
Donor: Mr. T. Hayes
A barbed and tanged arrowhead made from grey flint. Early Bronze Age.

Eltringham

Eltringham Farm, Northumberland
NZ 0714 6232
Cat. No. 1994.1
Donor: Mr. Harrison
A patinated flint blade (77mm long, 30mm across, 12mm thick) found during fieldwalking by Dr. S. Cousins. Late Upper Palaeolithic.

Ewart

Ewart Pit Alignments
NT 9534 3209 – 9610 3162
Cat. No. 1984.5.A
Donor: Mr. R. Miket
Refs: *PPS* 47 (1981): 137-146
Flints recovered during excavation on the Ewart pit alignments. Four flints, all light grey, including one broken blade tool with marginal retouch and a possible end segment of a plano-convex knife. Found associated with Grooved Ware. Late Neolithic-Early Bronze Age.

Felton

Felton
Cat. No. 1979.50
Donor: Mr. S. Beckensall
Collection of 14 flints discovered near Felton. Includes mostly light grey speckled flint pieces but also red-brown flint and medium grey flint. A tiny Mesolithic scraper, bladelets, occasional microliths and notched tools suggest an overall Late Mesolithic date for this assemblage.

Fenton

Fenton Wood
Cat. No. 1996.8
Bequest: Dr. J. Weyman
A total of 93 lithics comprising flint and non-flint material such as chert, quartz and agate. The collection includes mostly flakes with occasional scrapers, a gun flint and a fine barbed and tanged arrowhead. Mesolithic-Bronze Age.

Fenton Wood
Cat. No. 1996.8
Bequest: Dr. J. Weyman

NT 953 342	2 grey flint flakes.
NT 962 338	2 grey flint flakes and 2 burnt flint flakes.
NT 974 354	A dark grey flint scraper with abrupt retouch.
NT 954 346	A light grey flint scraper.
NT 973 343	3 brown and white flint flakes and 1 quartz flake.
NT 974 353	A broken barbed and tanged arrowhead, bladelet and broken blade. Grey-medium brown flint. Early Bronze Age.
NT 969 352	31 lithics including flint, agate, chert and quartz pieces. There are scrapers, flakes and blades. Mostly grey material and probably much of it Mesolithic. A single grey unprovenanced retouched flint flake – possibly a crude gun flint.

Flodden

Flodden, Near Milfield
Cat. No. 1970.13
Donor: Mrs. V. Rutherford
Refs: *Arch. News Bulletin* (Univ. of Newcastle) No. 10 (1971): 14
A single grey patinated flint bladelet, possibly a microlith, from near the hamlet of Flodden. Mesolithic.

Flotterton

NU 005 026
Cat. No. 1996.4.1
Bequest: Dr. J. Weyman
A single orange-grey flint bladelet core. Possibly Mesolithic.

Flotterton Area
NU 003 026
Cat. No. 1996.4.1
Bequest: Dr. J. Weyman
A dark grey flint bladelet and an orange-grey flint bladelet.

Ford

Cat. No. 1996.8
Bequest: Dr. J. Weyman

NT 9601 3707	A light grey flint barbed and tanged arrowhead. Early Bronze Age.
NT 962 358	A scraper and a flake made from light grey flint.
NT 963366	A grey flint scraper, possibly Mesolithic.
NT 957 378	3 grey flint flakes and a broken grey flint tanged tool.
NT 993 973	A broken dark grey flint flake.

Fowberry

NU 026 292
Cat. No. 1996.4.1
Bequest: Dr. J. Weyman
A collection of three flint flakes including an orange-grey, red-brown and light grey specimens.

Gallowhill

Gallowhill, Corbridge
NY 9977 6560
Cat. No. 1975.21
Donor: Dr. J. Weyman
Refs: *AA* 5th ser. 3 (1975): 219-221
Assemblage of 248 flints recovered during fieldwalking by Dr. J. Weyman in 1974-5. Includes microlithic flints, implements, cores and debitage. Mesolithic.

Gilchesters

Gilchesters
NZ 0625 7181
Cat. No. 1982.28
Donor: G.B. Dobinson
A single broken grey flint flake recovered during laying of gas pipeline near Gilchesters.

Gowanburn

Gowanburn River Camp
NY 661 902
Cat. No. 1998.1
Donor: Prof. G. Jobey
Refs: *AA* 5th ser. 16 (1988): 11-28
An assemblage of 48 lithics recovered from Jobey's excavations on the late Iron Age-Romano-British settlement. The assemblage includes artefacts of chert as well as flint. Pieces include microlith cores, flakes and blades. Probably mostly Mesolithic.

Grey Mare Hill Farm

Grey Mare Hill Farm
NZ 050 553
Cat. No. 1979.61
Donor: T. Heyes
A collection of 86 flints recovered during fieldwalking at Grey Mare Hill Farm including a broken barbed and tanged arrowhead, scrapers, retouched blade implements, a rod microlith and waste. Predominantly light grey flint with at least 28 burnt pieces. Late Mesolithic-Early Bronze Age.

Harbottle

Harbottle
Cat. No. 1979.62
Donor: T. Heyes
A light grey flint core from Harbottle with blade scars. Late Mesolithic-Early Neolithic date.

Harbottle Crags

Near abandoned farmhouse at Harbottle Crags
NT 923 028
Cat. No. 1976.8
Donor: Dr. Joan Weyman
A single struck flake of yellow cherty flint found during earth disturbance by the forestry commission.

Harehaugh Hillfort

Harehaugh Hillfort, Coquetdale
NY 970 998
Cat. No. 1999.3
Donor: P. Frodsham
Refs: *NA* 15/16 (1998): 87-108
2 flints found by Mr. P. Frodsham on ground surface inside Harehaugh Hillfort, probably associated with its Neolithic phase (see ref.). One is a light grey notched microlithic blade with broken tip and the other is a light grey squat blade tip with oblique (burin type) removal. Late Mesolithic-Neolithic.

Harthope Burn

Harthope Burn, Cheviots
Cat. No. 1984.4.A
Donor: Mr. R. Miket
A single light brown retouched flint blade from near the head of the Harthope Burn. Probably Neolithic.

Heddon Law

Heddon Law
NZ 144 695
Cat. No. 1933.10-13
Donor: W. Parker Brewis
Collection of 4 flints from Heddon Law including 1 grey blade, 1 grey possible end scraper, 1 broken grey cortical flake and 1 brown speckled broken core. Possibly Neolithic.

Hepburn Bell

NU 060 238
Cat. No. 1996.4.1
Bequest: Dr. J. Weyman
A grey flint flake and 2 quartz flakes.

High Shilford (see also Low Shilford)

High Shilford Farm
Cat. No. 1996.4.2
Bequest: Dr. J. Weyman
NZ 018 603
A collection of 10 lithics including fawn, light grey and red-brown flint flakes and blades, and a single dark grey chert flake.
NZ 019 601
A collection of 11 medium – light grey flints including flakes, scrapers and broken blades. Mesolithic.
NZ 019 605
A collection of 3 medium grey flint flakes.
NZ 025 607
A collection of 4 flints including a light grey blade, a ginger blade, a tiny ginger scraper and a patinated core. Mesolithic.
NZ 021 599
A collection of 3 flakes made from light grey flint.
NZ 039 607
A single light grey flake.

Holborn Moss

Holborn Moss, near Chatton
Cat. No. 1972.37
Donor: Mr. Smith
A large single flint platform core made from a medium grey flint with parallel sided blade scars. Probably Early Neolithic in date.

Holborn Moss, near Chatton
Cat. No. 1974.2
Assemblage of 20 flints nearly all broken by what appears to be plough damage. Five of the flints are burnt. Most of the flint is light grey with some speckled. Undiagnostic.

Holy Island

Sandham, Holy Island
NU 1342 4343
Cat. No. 1994.10
Donor: Dr. P. Dolukhanov and Prof. P. Fowler
A single dark purple chert blade found near to the Mesolithic site at Sandham. Probably Mesolithic.

Holy Island
Cat. No. 1956.165.1-2.A
A broken flint bladelet from the South side of Castle Rock, Holy Island. Mesolithic.

Housesteads

Housesteads Roman Fort
NY 790 688
Cat. No. 1956.151.12.A
3 flints from Housesteads.

Howick

Headland to North of Howick Burn
NU 25851660
Cat. No. 2002.15
Donor   Lord Howick
Ref: Waddington *et al* (2003)
An assemblage of more than 15,000 flints from an excavated Mesolithic structure dating to *c*.7800BC (Cal.) and from Early Bronze Age activity associated with a cist cemetery. Only perhaps a hundred or so of the flints are associated with the Bronze Age activity, most of the rest of the material having come from stratified deposits within the remains of a Mesolithic hut dwelling. The Mesolithic material is the single largest collection of flint from any site in Northumberland to date and this assemblage is in the process of being analysed ready for future publication. However, the following general comments can be made at this stage. The assemblage is dominated by debitage, as is typical of Mesolithic settlement sites but it also includes large quantities of microliths (particularly backed blades and scalene triangles) as well as cores, scrapers, piercers, burins and a variety of blade and flake tools. A collection of bevelled coarse stone tools was also recovered from inside the hut. All the flint is from locally available sources, being either beach pebble or glacial flint that can be picked up on the beach immediately below the site. This comes in a variety of colours though it includes predominantly grey, white, red-brown and ginger varieties. Relatively few of the pieces are patinated.

Fields adjacent to the Howick Mesolithic site
Field 1   NU 257 168
Field 2   NU 258 172
Field 3   NU 260 171
Field 4   NU 255 166
Field 5   NU 260 175
Field 6   NU 257 160
Field 7   NU 256 157
Cat. No. 2002.14
Ref: Waddington, C. 2002. Howick Archaeology Project, Northumberland. Fieldwalking Report. (unpub.)
Donor: Lord Howick
An assemblage of 244 lithics was recovered during systematic fieldwalking in 7 fields around the Mesolithic site. Most of the diagnostic lithics could be ascribed to a later Mesolithic narrow blade industry and correspond with the type of lithic material recovered from the excavation site. All the material that could be sourced was of local origin and can be found on the beach either

as beach pebbles washed in from the North Sea or as beach-rolled glacial nodules that have eroded out of the boulder clay before being washed back up on to the beach. A wide range of types are evident, ranging from primary flakes through to cores (mostly platform types for microlithic blade production), to scrapers, awls, edge-trimmed tools and a crescentic microlith. Concentrations of material could be evidenced and it is thought likely that other Mesolithic sites similar to the one excavated survive elsewhere on this neck of land by the Howick Burn.

Kennel Hall Knowe

Kennel Hall Knowe, North Tynedale
NY 667 898
Cat. No. 1979.26.A
Donor: Prof. G. Jobey
Ref: AA 5th ser. 6 (1978): 1-28
Assemblage of 168 flints and a heavily patinated polished stone axe recovered by Jobey during excavations on the Iron Age – Romano British settlement site. The assemblage includes pieces made from flint and chert. Types include 12 cores, core rejuvenation flakes, debitage, utilized flakes, 3 burins, 2 awls, 1 plano-convex knife with gloss, 1 denticulated knife with gloss, a leaf-shaped arrowhead and a hammer stone. Mesolithic – Neolithic. Other finds possibly associated include a cup-marked stone and beaker sherds.

Kielder Burn

Kielder Burn, Northumberland
Cat. No. 1956.323.A
Donor: Dr. E. Charlton
Ref: AJ 17 (1860): 60
A barbed and tanged arrowhead made from a yellow-brown flint. Late Neolithic-Early Bronze Age.

Kimmerston

NT 963 356
Cat. No. 1996.4.1
Bequest: Dr. J. Weyman
A grey flint core, a grey flint flake, an orange flint flake and a quartz flake.

Kirkhaugh

Kirkhaugh, Alston
Cat. No. 1936.13
Donor: Trustees of Greenwich Hospital
Refs: AA 4th ser. 13 (1936): 207
          AA 4th ser. 44 (1966): 219-20
          Tait, J. 1965, no. 31
Assemblage of 8 flints found during excavation of 2 cairns at Kirkhaugh. Other associated finds include a fine gold earring,

beaker fragments and rubbing stones. Flints include a barbed and tanged arrowhead and scraper. Late Neolithic-Early Bronze Age.

Kirkhill

West Hepple
NT 975 007
Cat. No. 1973.2
Donor: Mr. B. Howey
Refs: AA 5th ser. 2 (1974): 153
A total of 20 flints of which 4 are utilised. There is one triangular flint arrowhead measuring 28mm long with max. width 18mm, from the grave fill of skeleton 20 and a thumbnail scraper from the topsoil. Except for 2 calcined flints found within the collared urn all the others came from areas of subsequent disturbance. Quality and colour of the flint varies from milky grey to grey-black. Early Bronze Age.

Langleyford

Langleyford
Cat. No. 1991.15
Donor: Mr. E. W. Sockett
A white to light grey flint barbed and tanged arrowhead found in the Langleyford area. Early Bronze Age.

Lilburn

Lilburn Hill Farm
NU 013 256
Cat. No. 1890.9
Donor: Dr. Jas Hardy
Refs: AA 2nd ser. 13 (1890): 355
Fine thumbnail scraper found within cairnfield on Lilburn Hill which comprises cist burials containing at least one food vessel and one incense cup. Early Bronze Age.

West Lilburn
Cat. No. 1979.37.A
Donor: Prof. G. Jobey
An assemblage of 18 Early Bronze Age flints discovered during excavations by Prof. G. Jobey and found in relation to a fragmentary, though fine, food vessel. The lithics include two quartz flakes and a chert flake with the rest flint of a light grey or milky-coloured variety. They include three scrapers, a retouched flake and flake pieces.

Longframlington

Longframlington
Cat. No. 1938.36
Donor: Mr. A.R. Robson
Refs: PSAN 4th ser. 8 (1939): 242
A single fawn-coloured broken flake.

Low Farnham

NU 978 029
Cat. No. 1996.4.1
Bequest: Dr. J. Weyman
A collection of 4 grey flint flakes, one of which is edge-trimmed.

Low Shilford

Low Shilford, Tyne Valley
NZ 032 615
Cat. Nos. 1982.8, 1982.13
Donor: Trustees of the Bywell Estates
Collection of 33 flints recovered during laying of gas pipeline. Mostly waste flakes. A variety of material but mostly light grey flint, some patinated. Undiagnostic.

Low Shilford
NZ 031 617
Cat. No. 1985.30
Donor: Dr. J. Weyman
Refs: *AA* 5th ser. 8 (1980): 159-61
Assemblage of 192 flints from a variety of locations in the Low Shilford area recovered by surface collection. The assemblage is dominated by blade forms, many of which are broken. Most of the pieces are flakes, blades and debitage but also includes cores, core fragments, retouched flakes and blades, scrapers, at least two microliths and a knife. The flint is mostly light grey glacial material but also includes shades of pink and occasional pieces of high quality dark grey nodular flint. Predominantly later Mesolithic pieces with possibly some later material.

Luckermoorhouse

Luckermoorhouse
Cat Nos. 1927.139.5, 1927.139.6
Donor: Mr. F. Buckley
Refs: *PSAN* 3rd ser. 10 (1923): 271
PSAN 4th ser. 3 (1929): 93
2 barbed and tanged arrowheads found between Twyzell and North Sandyford. One is a grey mottled flint, exceptionally well made. The other is a pale grey flint. Late Neolithic-Early Bronze Age.

Luckermoorhouse
Cat. No. 1927.139
Donor: Mr. F. Buckley
Collection of lithics found as surface finds from Alnmouth, Budle Bay, Ross Links and Luckermoorhouse. 6 flints comprising light grey-speckled flint of which 3 are patinated. They include a platform core and a flake core for microlithic blank detachments, together with a utilised blade and a small isosceles triangular point microlith and two flakes. Mesolithic.

Mainsbank

Mainsbank
NZ 0700 07284
Cat. No. 1982.22
Donor: G.R. Stoppard
A single flint flake found during laying of gas pipes.

Manside Cross

Manside Cross
NY 984 921
Cat. No. 1979.38.A
Donor: Prof. G. Jobey
2 flints found during Jobey's excavations on the Manside Cross Romano-British settlement site including one microlithic bladelet with a parallel-sided blade scar on the dorsal surface and a larger flake with marginal retouch.

Matfen

High Houses Farm
NZ 0491 7007
Cat. No. 1982.25
Donor: C.G. Urwin
Collection of 14 flints from High Houses Farm, Matfen, during excavation for gas pipeline. Includes a superb used plano-convex knife and two scrapers as well as a variety of flakes, some retouched, and blades. Mostly light grey flint but also orange-grey and red-brown flint.

Thornham Hill, Matfen
NZ 0524 7049
Cat. No. 1982.26
Donor: G & I Egglestone and Sons
A single flint recovered during laying of gas pipeline.

Matfen
Cat. No. 1996.4.2
Bequest: Dr. J. Weyman
NZ 036 709
A dark grey flint core and 4 light grey flint flakes.
NZ 028 708
2 grey flint flakes.
NZ 041 697
2 grey flint flakes and 1 brown flint flake.
NZ 043 694
A collection of 7 flints including an excellent example of a leaf-shaped arrowhead made from purple flint, a red-brown scraper and blade segment plus grey and yellow-brown flakes. Neolithic.

Milfield

Hay Farm
Cat. No. 1967.4.A
Donor: Mr. J.T. Moore
A barbed and tanged arrowhead found below the corner of a large stone slab that covered black soil with a layer of stones along the side (burial pit with capstone?). Late Neolithic-Early Bronze Age.

Milfield Village
Cat. No. 1984.8.A
Donor: Mr. R. Miket
A single flint axe. Neolithic.

Whitton Hill, north of Milfield village
NT 933 347
Cat. No. 1994.9
Donor: Tyne and Wear Museum Service
Ref: *PPS* 51 (1985): 137-148
7 flints from Miket's excavations on the Whitton Hill Early Bronze Age hengiform and ring ditch. They include a fine fabricator made from imported nodular flint together with a broken blade segment, a chert rejuvenation flake, an edge-trimmed flake, two flint flakes and an agate flake. Late Neolithic-Early Bronze Age.

Whitton Hill, north of Milfield village
NT 9265 3475
Cat. No. 1996.8
Bequest: Dr. J. Weyman
A light grey flint blade and one red agate chip. Undiagnostic.

Milfield Basin Area
NT910325 - NT966366
Cat. No. 1999.5
Donor: Dr. C. Waddington
Refs: Waddington 1999a
An assemblage of 666 lithics were recovered during a systematic fieldwalking programme over the Milfield basin. A transect extending over 600ha. was walked across the basin from a watershed in the Cheviots to a watershed on the sandstone escarpment. A wide range of raw materials is represented in the assemblage including chipped agate, quartz, chert, volcanic material and flint. Most of the material recovered appears to have been utilised, indicating a parsimonious attitude to lithic discard. The fieldwalking assemblage includes cores, scrapers, arrowheads/points and microliths as well as borers, knives, blades, flakes, unclassified implements and test pieces. Mesolithic, Neolithic and Bronze Age lithics are represented in the assemblage which also includes a broken flint tranchet axe blade, a sandstone axe and a Cheviot andesite stone axe. A further 99 lithics were also recovered from the test-pitting programme.

A second phase of fieldwalking took place during 2000 resulting in the recovery of 613 lithics with an additional 21 recovered from the test pits. The assemblage contains 41 bashed lumps, 127 cores and over 380 flakes and blades in addition to a variety of retouched and utilised flakes and blades, at least 8 microliths, a burin, 14 scrapers, a barbed and tanged arrowhead and a gun flint. Most of the lithics are made from non-flint locally available material including agate and chert with quartz also utilised. Most of the diagnostic material is late Mesolithic in character but occasional later pieces are included, such as the barbed and tanged arrowhead. Mesolithic-Early Bronze Age.

Milfield Demesne Farm
NT 936 337
Cat. No. 1996.9
Bequest: Dr. J. Weyman
A total of 79 lithics from around Milfield, much of which is non-flint material. The collection includes pieces of chert, agate, quartz, flint and jasper. Although mostly flakes, there are scrapers, cores and some blades. Probably mostly Mesolithic.

Milfield Henge Sites
Cat. No. 1996.11.1, 1996.11.2, 1996.11.3
Donor: Prof. A. Harding
Refs: *PPS* 47 (1981): 87-135
49 Flints from Harding's excavations in the henge monuments of the Milfield Basin including Milfield North (NT 934 348), Milfield South (NT 939 335) and Yeavering (NT 928 303). Includes a cache of honey-grey barbed and tanged flint arrowheads from one of the Milfield North shafts as well as light grey scrapers and a range of flakes. Late Neolithic-Early Bronze Age.

Morpeth

Morpeth
NZ 2450 5463
Cat. No. 1996.4.4
Bequest: Dr. J. Weyman
A single dark grey flint scraper with abrupt retouch found on a ploughed field surface in a sandy area.

Morpeth
NZ 2086
Cat No. 1957.278.A
Donor: none recorded
Highly polished grey flint axe head with a central flaw creating a concentric circle design. This flaw may be the reason why the piece was selected although much of it would be covered when the haft was in position.

Morralee

NY 7995 6405
Cat. No. 1996.4.1
Bequest: Dr. J. Weyman
A single broken grey flint flake.

Newbiggin

Element Head, Newbiggin
NZ 319 880
Cat. No. 1979.59
Donor: T. Heyes
A collection of 166 flints of various colours in a stratified context from a cliff section at Element Head (drawing lodged with collection). Includes a quartzite hammer stone, microliths, cores, retouched flakes and much debitage. Wide variety of flint including red-brown, light grey and dark grey. Late Mesolithic date.

New House Farm

New House Farm
NZ 0310 5373
Cat. No. 1982.14
Donor: Trustees of the Minsteracres Estates
A single chert core found during laying of gas pipe line.

North Seaton

Sandy Lane West, North Seaton
Cat. No. 1979.57
Donor: Mr. Percy
Assemblage of 709 lithics including one microlith, scrapers and cores of Mesolithic date and one leaf-shaped arrowhead, plus scrapers, awls, knife/fabricator and a barbed and tanged arrowhead of Neolithic-Early Bronze Age date. There are good examples of platform blade cores. Much of the material is patinated. A wide range of material is present including light grey flint, orange flint and red-brown flint most likely from local sources. There are also a substantial number of quartz pieces. This collection would repay further analysis.

North Seaton
Cat. No. 1996.4.4
Bequest: Dr. J. Weyman
Collection of 54 lithics collected during fieldwalking, including some collected by Heyes. Some of the nodular material is probably ballast. However, other pieces, predominantly of glacial flint, include cores, flakes and blades and some good examples of scrapers, most with abrupt retouch suggesting a Mesolithic date.

Old Ridley

Tyne Valley
Cat. No. 1996.4.2
Bequest: Dr. J. Weyman
NZ 053 605
3 flints including 1 core and 1 flake that are heavily patinated and a light grey flake.
NZ 0485 6085
A burnt flint and a flake.
NZ 053 605 and 0500 6055
A collection of 6 broken yellow-brown flints including 1 grey core.

Otterburn

Featherwood Farm, Otterburn
Cat. No. 1987.6
Donor: R.W. Fairhurst
A single flint blade found 1 mile north-east of Featherwood Farm on Otterburn Ranges in 1978.

Otterburn
NY 915 917
Cat. No. 1996.5.1
Bequest: Dr. J. Weyman
A single light grey flint flake.

Ponteland

Braid Hill NZ 16 70
Cat. No. 1921.12
Donor: Dr. J.A. Smythe
A possible palaeolith. It is a large bi-facially worked hand-axe type made from very poor quality flint/chert with many quartzite impurities. Interestingly, this lithic is thought to be of Purbeck chert and could, therefore, be an imported collector's piece and not originally from the Ponteland area.

Powburn

NU 06 16
Cat. No. 1996.4.1
Bequest: Dr. J. Weyman
A single quartz scraper with abrupt retouch. Undiagnostic.

Red House

Red House, Beaufront, near Corbridge
NY 972 651
Cat. No. 1961.19.14
Refs: *AA* 4th ser. 37 (1959): 85-176
A single flint flake.

Riding Mill

West Plantation, Dipton House, Riding Mill
NY 98 60
Cat. No. 1935.24
Donor: Miss B. Burn
A single flint flake found 6 inches below the surface in plantation.

Ripley Hall

Ripley Hall Plantation
Cat. No. 1983.22.A
Donor: Prof. G. Jobey
4 flints recovered during excavations which also yielded a bone ring, pin and pottery.

Ross Links

Ross Links
Cat. No. 1927.139
Donor: F. Buckley
5 lithics found as surface finds from Alnmouth, Budle Bay, Ross Links and Luckermoorhouse. Mesolithic-Bronze Age.

Ross Links
Cat. No. 1927.139.9
Donor: Mrs. F. Buckley
Refs: *PSAN* 4th ser. 3 (1929): 92
A single thumbnail scraper made from yellow-grey mottled flint. Early Bronze Age.

Rothbury

Rothbury
Cat. No. 1932.14
Donor: Wilfred Hall (ex Dippie Dixon Collection)
Refs: *PSAN* 4th ser. 5 (1933): 233-236
A collection of 156 flints including a gun flint from Low Farnham Farm and areas around Rothbury. A fine collection including at least 11 leaf-shaped arrowheads, 5 barbed and tanged arrowheads, knives, Late Mesolithic scrapers, blade tools and cores. A wide variety of flint types including light grey speckled, medium grey, red-brown and ginger. Mesolithic – Early Bronze Age. This is an important collection which would repay a fuller analysis. The collection also includes two perforated amber toggles from Simonside (on display) that may be belt terminals (see also ref. in *AA* 1966 4th ser. 44: 217-219).

Ward's Hill, Rothbury
Cat. No. 1937.7.1-3
Donor: W.P. Hedley
Refs: *PSAN* 4th ser. 8 (1939): 66
Collection of 11 flints found during quarrying including a light

grey barbed and tanged arrowhead, scrapers, a blade with marginal retouch and a whetstone together with Beaker fragments. Neolithic-Early Bronze Age.

Rothbury
Cat. No. 1948.3
A single grey black flint scraper.

Roughting Lynn

Roughting Lynn, near Kimmerston
NT 983 368
Cat. No. 1985.10
Donor: Miss J.M. Jackson
A single grey flint knife with neat flaking and invasive retouch. Neolithic-Early Bronze Age.

Rudchester

Cat. No. 1983.26
Donor: R. Moorwood
A single thumbnail scraper recovered by surface collection. Early Bronze Age.

Shadon Hill

Cat. No. 1979.64
Donor: T. Heyes
Collection of 4 flints from Shadon Hill. Two light grey, one dark grey flakes and a tiny white chip. Undiagnostic.

Shaw House

NZ 0307 6386
Cat. No. 1982.7
Donor: Trustees of Viscount Allendale's Settled Estates.
Single flint broken bladelet segment found near Shaw House during laying of gas pipeline. Lightly patinated, probably Mesolithic.

Simonside

Simonside, near Rothbury
Cat. No. 1889.23.3
Refs: *PSAN* 2nd ser. 4 (1891): 169 and 172
AA 2nd ser. 15 (1892): 23
A single dark grey flint scraper found embedded in a mass of cremated bone in a cinerary urn from a barrow 120 yards north of Willies Cairn on Spital Hill.

Spindlestone

Spindlestone, near Belford
Cat. No. 1924.21
Donor: Mr. F. Buckley
Refs: *PSAN* 4th ser. 1 (1925): 298
      AA 4th ser. 1 (1925): 42-47

An assemblage of Mesolithic flints totalling 358 pieces discovered during Buckley's excavations at Spindlestone. Includes a large quantity of debitage and 9 microliths. The microliths are nearly all narrow blade forms. Although the 4 geometric rods (including 2 with points) are probably Late Mesolithic a large obliquely blunted patinated microlith is potentially of Early Mesolithic date. There are also cores with microlithic blade scars on recycled patinated pieces suggestive of Earlier Mesolithic or Palaeolithic use of the pieces prior to the Late Mesolithic recycling. There are also scrapers but most of the assemblage consists of debitage (236 pieces). This collection would benefit from a more detailed evaluation.

Stocksfield

New Ridley Road, Stocksfield
Cat. No. 1933.6
Donor: W. J. Bulmer
Refs: *PSAN* 4th ser. 6 (1935): 19-20

A large flint flake found a few inches below a gravel path at house called 'Shanklin' on New Ridley Road, Stocksfield. It has limited marginal retouch at the distal end and evidence of utilization along its edges. It is made from a dark grey, probably nodular, flint. Undiagnostic.

Thirlings

Thirlings, near Ewart
NT 956 320 (centres on)
Cat. No. 1996.7
Bequest: Dr. J. Weyman

A substantial collection of 1,018 lithics from Thirlings and its environs in the Milfield basin, mostly picked up by fieldwalking. A notebook and files with locational information, identifications and illustrations accompanies them. The assemblage contains a range of material belonging to Mesolithic, Neolithic and Bronze Age traditions. There are many fine pieces as well as good examples of bashed lumps of quartz. Other than that there are fine examples of scrapers, leaf-shaped arrowheads, barbed and tanged arrowheads, a transverse arrowhead, a small sickle blade, retouched blades, a burin, possible microliths, platform cores and a good example of a microburin as well as flakes, blades and a gunflint. The raw material used is particularly wide-ranging, as is typical for this area, and includes chert, quartz, agate and volcanic glass as well as flint. Most of the flint is light grey with occasional pieces of dark grey nodular flint.

Thirston

West Moor Farm
NZ 175 988
Cat. No. 1996.4.3
Bequest: Dr. J. Weyman

A total of 356 lithics collected by fieldwalking. Includes flint and chert pieces. Wide range of flint including red-brown, fawn, orange-brown, light grey and a lot of burnt material. Types include cores, microliths, bladelets, blades and flakes. Late Mesolithic-Early Neolithic.

Threestoneburn

Threestoneburn House
Cat. No. 1978.5
Donor: Forestry Commission

One flint flake made from light grey speckled flint.

Thrunton

NU 090 072
Cat. No. 1996.4.1
Bequest: Dr. J. Weyman

A single burnt flint scraper.

Tosson

Tosson Tower Farm
NU 029 011
Cat. No. 1996.4.1
Bequest: Dr. J. Weyman

A collection of 11 light grey and red-brown flints that includes flakes and blades.

Trewitt

NU 006 067
Cat. No. 1996.4.1
Bequest: Dr. J. Weyman

A collection of 62 flints including flakes, microliths and bladelets made from light grey material and 2 quartz flakes.

Trewitt Steads
NU 006 066
Cat. No. 1983.7
Donor: Mr. E.C. Gair

Collection of 39 flints found by T. Gates during fieldwalking in field west of Trewitt Steads. Includes Late Mesolithic material including a scraper, blades, microlith and burnt cores. Mostly light grey speckled flint and burnt pieces.

Wallhouses

Wallhouses Area
NZ 0425 6832
Cat. No. 1982.10
Donor: J.E. Moffit
A single flint found during laying of gas pipeline.

Wallhouses Area
NZ 0438 6862
Cat. No. 1982.11
Donor: Matfen Settled Estates
A single flint scraper found during laying of gas pipeline.

Warden

Warden, near Hexham
NY 906 664
Cat. No. 1978.23
Donor: Mr. J. Thomson
Collection of 174 flints from the Warden area. Includes at least 14 cores, most of which have microlithic bladelet scars, and there is a classic single platform pyramidal core and narrow blade microlith. The majority of the assemblage is debitage and includes many flakes and blades. The material is mostly light grey speckled flint of glacial origin with occasional dark grey, orange-grey and red-brown glacial flint. The assemblage is generally Late Mesolithic in date.

Warden Hill
NY 911 664
Cat. No. 1999.2
Donor: Dr. C. Waddington
An assemblage of 6 lithics found during casual surface collection on the ploughed field adjacent to the ringwork which contains a 'long mound' of either natural or manmade/enhanced origin. As it was realised that there were many lithics in the ploughsoil of this field the donor decided not to collect any more as systematic sampling of the field is required. There are 5 flint pieces and one quartz piece. The quartz tool is a scraper while the flint pieces include 3 light grey flakes, 1 burnt core and a burnt blade. Mesolithic-Neolithic.

Warden Hill
NY 904 669 and other nearby locations
Cat. No. 1999.19
Donor: Mr. S. Beckensall
A total of 58 flints from four different findspots collected during fieldwalking. Although largely flakes, blades and debitage the assemblage contains 1 triangular microlith and a steeply retouched Mesolithic scraper. Most of the flint is of a light grey colour with some darker grey. A number of the pieces are patinated and many have cortex surviving, indicating a glacial origin for most of this material. All diagnostic material is Late Mesolithic. Published in the Hexham Historian.

Warden Area
NY 9135 6821
Cat. No. 1996.4.2
Bequest: Dr. J. Weyman
1 grey flint blade and a quartz chip.

Warrenford

Warrenford, Northumberland
NU 133 301
Cat. No. 1979.68
Donor: T. Heyes
A single light grey flint flake. Undiagnostic. Found just off the line of the new by-pass.

Wellhope

Wellhope, near Edlingham
NU 115 066 and NU 115 059
Cat. No. 1979.60
Donor: T. Heyes
Collection of 43 flints found near the farmhouse and to its west. Includes occasional scrapers and cores but mostly waste flakes. Predominantly light grey speckled flint but also some ginger coloured, red-brown and dark grey flint.

West Moorhouse

West Moorhouse
NZ 0475 6986
Cat. No. 1982.9
Donor: Matfen Settled Estates
Collection of 300 flints found during laying of gas pipeline.

West Moorhouse
NZ 0442 6936
Cat. No. 1982.24
Donor: Matfen Settled Estates
A single flint recovered from near West Moorhouse during laying of gas pipeline.

Woodburn

Woodburn
Cat. No. 1932.74
Donor: R.C. and W.P. Hedley
Refs: *PSAN* 4th ser. 5 (1933): 329
A single worked flint point.

Woodhorn

NZ 295 879
Cat. No. 1996.4.4
Bequest: Dr. J. Weyman
A total of 21 flints collected by fieldwalking. Includes a wide range of material such as light grey, medium grey, red-brown and ginger flint. The dark grey flint is possibly ballast. The collection includes 6 scrapers, 1 broken scraper, a core, blades and flakes. Mesolithic.

Wooler

Haugh Head
Cat. No. 1946.25
Donor: Dr. E.F. Collingwood
Refs: *AA* 4th ser. 26 (1948): 47-54
An assemblage of 5 flints recovered from a cist that also contained a complete food vessel and cremated bone. Includes a pointed tool (possible spearhead), oblique arrowhead and 4 small worked flints. Early Bronze Age. The cist was located on top of a prominent knoll at the back of Haugh Head farmhouse on the east side of the modern A697 trunk road.

Wooperton

NU 045 205
Cat. No. 1996.4.1
Bequest: Dr. J. Weyman
A single grey flint flake.

Wylam

Area West of Wylam
Cat. No. 1956.347.A
Donor: Mr. W.A. Wright
Collection of 35 flints found to the west of Wylam. Predominantly light grey flint with some burnt pieces. Mostly flakes and debitage with blade segments and a broken retouched blade segment. Mesolithic.

COUNTY DURHAM

Allenheads

Bell's Quarry
NY 852 422
Cat. No. 1938.35
Donor: Mr. J.A. Walton
Refs: *PSAN* 4th ser. 8 (1939): 242
An assemblage of 49 lithics from the neighbourhood of Bell's Quarry on the road between Wearheads and Allenheads was given to the Museum in 1938. A second batch from the same area was deposited in 1939. The collection includes one broken scalene triangle Late Mesolithic microlith, an unusual squat point microlith together with a chert platform core, flakes and blades. Mesolithic.

Blanchland Area

NY 932 448
Cat. No. 1996.5.1
Bequest: Dr. J. Weyman
A single orange flint flake.

Brandon

NU 04 17
Cat. No. 1996.5.1
Bequest: Dr. J. Weyman
2 dark grey flint flakes and an orange-brown flake.

Chester-le-Street

Chester-le-Street Roman Fort
Cat. No. 1991.17
Donor: E.W. Sockett
A single light grey broken flint blade found on the spoil heap at Chester-le-Street Roman fort.

Durhamfield

NZ 0566 5002
Cat. No. 1982.23
Donor: Mr. E. Taylor
A single dark grey broken flint flake found during laying of gas pipeline near Durhamfield.

Ebchester

NZ 093 573
Cat. No. 1996.5.1
Bequest: Dr. J. Weyman
A single light grey broken flint core.

Ebchester
NZ 096 557
Cat. No. 1996.5.1

Bequest: Dr. J. Weyman
A single light grey broken flint blade.

Edmundbyres

Cat. No. 1932.90.H
Refs: *PSAN* 4th ser. 5 (1933): 334
Collection of 10 flints including a Late Mesolithic tiny scraper, a broken notched blade segment together with a long unretouched blade and seven flakes. Most of the flints are light grey and Late Mesolithic; however, the very heavily patinated flake with marginal retouch is probably considerably earlier. This piece is also a different kind of flint. The smoothing of its edges suggests it has been rolled and transported, which hints towards a date prior to the Postglacial.

Eshwinning

Cat. No. 1952.6
Donor: R. Walters
A single broken barbed and tanged arrowhead made from orange-brown flint. Late Neolithic-Early Bronze Age.

Finchale Nab

NZ 299 468
Cat. No. 1935.21
Donor: Mr. H. Preston
Refs: *PSAN* 4th ser. 7 (1937): 118
Collection of flints from Finchale Nab. Mesolithic.

CLEVELAND

Hartlepool

NZ 50 32
Cat. No. 1996.5.1
Bequest: Dr. J. Weyman
A single dark grey flint flake, probably from ballast.

Ladiesgillbridge

Teesdale.
Cat. No. 1996.5.1
Bequest: Dr. J. Weyman
A single grey-brown flint flake.

Seaton Carew

Seaton Carew, West Hartlepool
NZ 52 29/30
Cat. No. 1883.10.1-15
A collection of material from Seaton Carew including 6 flints.

TYNE AND WEAR

Blackfell Hill

NZ 286 579
Cat. No. 1979.63
Donor: T. Heyes
2 flints: one a snapped, possibly edge-trimmed, blade segment made from light honey-coloured flint and the second a small grey flint flake.

Blakelaw

Cat. No. 2001.17
Donor: Robinson Library
A single light grey flint scraper with abrupt retouch. Possibly Mesolithic

Blaydon

Stargate
NZ 1662 6298
Cat. No. 1958.7.A
Donor: Rev. L.T. Johnson
Refs: Miket 1984, 25
An opaque light grey flint knife found on the western tip of McAlpine sand quarry, Bewes Hills, Stargate amongst the top soil.

Gosforth

Beaumont Street allotments, Newcastle upon Tyne
Cat. No. 1958.5
Donor: Mr. A. Coulston

A flint spear point found in the Beaumont Street allotments near to electric car sheds. Early Bronze Age.

Longbenton

Cat. No. 1981.2
Donor: Mrs. C. Bunn
A broken flint microlith found in the back garden of the donor. Mesolithic.

Newcastle

Benton
Cat. No. 1932.96
Donor: The Hancock Museum
A single light grey edge-trimmed flake found in gravel for garden path. Gravel came from Bridgeport.

Black Gate, City Centre
NZ 2503 6380
Cat. No. 1933.35
Donor: Miss Norah Balls
Refs: Miket 1984: 43
A serrated flint blade made from brown flint found between the Black Gate and the Railway line.

Black Gate, City Centre
Cat. No. 1986.14
Donor: Newcastle City Council
Total of 7 flints found during 1986 excavations at the Black Gate when it was found that they were already marked and appeared to have escaped from the Black Gate Museum during the move to the present museum site. Weyman believed these might be those donated to The Society of Antiquaries of Newcastle by Mr. G. Burnett from Lake Erie, Canada.

Byker, Norbury Grove
Cat. No. 1972.39
Donor: Mrs. Tait
Refs: Miket 1984: 43
2 burnt flint flakes found in garden.

Jesmond
Cat. No. 1956.310.A
Refs: 1984: 36
Collection of 4 grey flints including a large cortical flake, a core, a broken heavily patinated scraper and a heavily patinated flake. The latter two are possibly Palaeolithic.

South Gosforth, Rectory Grove
Cat. No. 1981.3
Donor: Mrs. G. McCombie
A total of 26 lithic pieces, many of them nodules and all very heavily patinated including light grey and orange flint. Mainly flakes though nothing diagnostic. There are 3 burnt pieces and one agate piece, possibly chipped.

Ryton

Cat. No. 1970.1.A.(A-J)
Donor: Mr. W.A. Cocks
A collection of 371 flints from the Ryton area with donor's notebook containing inventory of the flints with map showing findspots. Mesolithic-Bronze Age, though there are no microliths and much of the material is likely to be Bronze Age. Includes many cores for microlith blank production. Mainly light grey speckled flint. The Cocks Collection contains a wide range of pieces including various types of scrapers (thumbnail, side, end, hollow), cores, blade tools, arrowheads (leaf-shaped and barbed and tanged), awls, knives and fabricators. Also present are gun flints that could relate to the battle of Newburn in 1640. Most of the tools from the Cocks Collection are drawn and described in the accompanying archive; a recent database by P. Cook describes each find and her notes include information on each of the 15 'sites', or collection areas, visited by Cocks.

Emma Colliery, Ryton
NZ 1445 6380
Cat. No. 1958.8.9
Donor: Rev. L.T. Johnson
Refs: *AA* 4th ser. 44 (1966): 246

2 flint arrowheads discovered as surface finds in a ploughed field behind Emma Colliery. Neolithic.

South Shields

South Shields Area
Cat. No. 1923.12
Donor: R. Blair
Refs: *PSAN* 2nd ser. 3 (1887): 3
 PSAN 4th ser. 1 (1925): 128
A single flint spear point found on a ballast heap, almost certainly imported from southern England, made from very high quality dark grey flint. Very fine piece with invasive retouch on both surfaces. Late Neolithic.

South Shields Area
Cat. No. 1956.128.62.A
A single flint scraper with fine abrupt retouch made from a medium grey flint. Mesolithic.

Swalwell

Swalwell Area
Cat. No. 1988.42
Donor: Mrs. J.H. Smith
A single medium grey flint blade with broken distal tip.

Tynemouth

Tynemouth Priory
NZ 374 695
Cat. No. 1979.22.3
Donor: Prof. G. Jobey
Refs: *AA* 4th ser. 45 (1967): 90
 Miket 1984: 82
Small collection of flints, including struck flakes and two gun flints, recovered during Jobey's excavations at Tynemouth priory and castle.

Throckley

Dewley Farm, Throckley
NZ 1605 6827
Cat. No. 1978.30
Donor: Mrs. D. Cutts
Refs: Miket 1984: 17
A single hollow-based flint arrowhead with fine ripple flaking, Clarke's Class G. Found during ploughing. Late Neolithic.

Dewley Hill Kaim (or barrow), Throckley
NZ 1603 6802
Cat. No. 1935.22
Donor: Mr. H. Preston
Refs: Miket 1984: 15
Assemblage of 6 flints.

Dewley Hill Tumulus (or glacial mound), Throckley
NZ 160 683
Cat. Nos. 1991.20.1, 1991.20.2
Donor: Dr. J. Weyman and Mr. Lawson
Assemblage of 180 flints collected from the Dewley Hill mound and surrounding fields during fieldwalking. Mesolithic-Neolithic.

Walbottle

NZ 166 664
Cat. No. 1970.15
Donor: Miss. R.B. Harbottle and Mr. D. Peel
Refs: *Archaeological News Bulletin* (University of Newcastle) No.7 Jan.1970: 12
A fawn coloured broken flint from a retouched tanged tool. Neolithic-Bronze Age.

West Denton

West Denton, Newcastle
NZ 190 661
Cat. No. 1961.4
Donor: Mr. J. Armstrong
Refs: *AA* 4th ser. 41 (1963): 220
 Miket 1984: 16
A single leaf-shaped arrowhead found in donor's garden. Early Neolithic.

Westerhope

2 Trafford Walk, Westerhope
NZ 1911 6713
Cat. No. 1956.137.A
Donor: Mr. D. Bell
Refs: Miket 1984, 17
A grey-brown translucent flint arrowhead with secondary flaking along edges and missing tip. Found in builder's upcast from house foundations in donor's garden.

Westerhope
2 Kelso Close, Westerhope
NZ 1845 6759
Cat. No. 1974.7
Donor: Mr. M.J. Taylor
Refs: Miket 1984, 15
A barbed and tanged arrowhead with one broken barb made from a brown flint found in the donor's garden. Late Neolithic-Early Bronze Age.

Whickham

Cat. No. 1988.42
Donor: Mrs. J.M.. Smith
A single light grey flint blade.

YORKSHIRE

Butterwick

SE 993 702
Cat. No. 1996.3.9
Bequest: Dr. J. Weyman
7 grey flints including a blade core, end scraper and broken flakes and blades. Mesolithic-Early Neolithic.

Cat Babbleton

Cat Babbleton, Yorkshire Wolds
Cat. No. 1996.3.7
Bequest: Dr. J. Weyman
A total of 34 flints collected by fieldwalking. Assemblage dominated by light grey flint which includes scrapers, retouched blade tools, microliths and flakes. Late Mesolithic.

Cold Kirby

SE 514 847
Cat. No. 1996.3.9
Bequest: Dr. J. Weyman
12 flints including 11 grey and 1 honey coloured piece consisting of broken flakes and a broken backed blade.

Danby Moor

Danby Moor, North York Moors
Cat. No. 1972.9
Donor: Mrs. W. Percy Hedley
Single triangular flint tool with retouch along both long edges and broken point.

Duggleby Howe

SE 87 67
Cat. No. 1996.3.9
Bequest: Dr. J. Weyman
2 grey flints including an edge-trimmed grey flake and a retouched blade. Neolithic.

Foxholes

Foxholes, various grid references
Cat. No. 1996.3.3
Bequest: Dr. J. Weyman

TA 018 738	28 flints
TA 012 742	7 flints
TA 006 734	17 flints
TA 003 734	8 flints
TA 001 732	24 flints
TA 001 734	32 flints
TA 008 714	14 flints
TA 006 730	15 flints
TA 01 73	21 flints

A total of 135 flints collected by fieldwalking. The assemblage comprises predominantly light grey mottled flint. It includes cores, blades, blade tools, scrapers, microliths and burins. In general, a Late Mesolithic assemblage worthy of reassessment.

Foxholes
TA 01 73
Cat. No. 1996.3.11
Bequest: Dr. J. Weyman
3 grey flint flakes all of which appear to have been utilised.

Foxholes
TA 01 73
Cat. No. 1996.3.12
Bequest: Dr. J. Weyman
2 light grey flint scrapers.

Foxholes
TA 01 73
Cat. No. 1996.3.13
Bequest: Dr. J. Weyman
6 grey flint flakes, some broken.

Ganton Wold

Ganton Wold
TA 012 736 and TA 01 74
Cat. No. 1996.3.6
Bequest: Dr. J. Weyman
A total of 17 flints collected by fieldwalking from two findspots. An assemblage of light and dark grey flints including a steeply retouched scraper, retouched blade tools, blades, bladelets and flakes. Late Mesolithic.

Ganton Wold
TA 01 74
Cat. No. 1996.3.11
Bequest: Dr. J. Weyman
5 grey flints including 1 burnt scraper, 3 bladelets and a flake. Probably Mesolithic.

Ganton Wold
TA 01 74
Cat. No. 1996.3.12
Bequest: Dr. J. Weyman
A single pale grey small flint scraper.

Ganton Wold
TA 01 74
Cat. No. 1996.3.13
Bequest: Dr. J. Weyman
3 grey flint flakes.

Helperthorpe

Yorkshire Wolds
Cat. No. 1996.3.5
Bequest: Dr. J. Weyman

SE 949 717	13 flints
SE 970 685	6 flints
SE 970 788	26 flints
SE 96 70	5 flints

A total of 50 flints collected by fieldwalking from different findspots. Collection dominated by light grey flint, some of which patinated. Includes blades, cores, and microliths. Late Mesolithic.

Helperthorpe
SE 97 68
Cat. No. 1996.3.11
Bequest: Dr. J. Weyman
A single patinated broken retouched blade segment.

Helperthorpe
SE 97 68
Cat. No. 1996.3.12
Bequest: Dr. J. Weyman
3 small grey scrapers, 1 with abrupt retouch and two of them patinated. Possibly Mesolithic.

Helperthorpe Pasture
SE 96 70
Cat. No. 1996.3.13
Bequest: Dr. J. Weyman
A single grey flint flake.

Heslerton

West and East Heslerton
Cat. No. 1996.3.8
Bequest: Dr. J. Weyman

SE 912 738	4 flints
SE 909-913 735-7	19 flints
SE 917 725	3 flints
SE 93 73	1 flint

A total of 27 flints collected during fieldwalking from various findspots. Mostly light grey and white flint. Includes microliths, scrapers, cores and retouched blade tools. Late Mesolithic.

Luttons

Luttons Various Grid References
Cat. No. 1996.3.2
Bequest: Dr. J. Weyman

SE 930 709	20 flints
SE 939 704	8 flints
SE 93 70	7 flints

A total of 28 flints collected by fieldwalking from various findspots. Mostly light grey flint, much of which has light patina development. Includes broken blade tools and regular cores with microlithic bladelet removals. Late Mesolithic.

Luttons
SE 93 70
Cat. No. 1996.3.11
Bequest: Dr. J. Weyman
1 grey retouched flint flake.

Luttons
SE 93 70
Cat. No. 1996.3.12
Bequest: Dr. J. Weyman
A single pale grey retouched flint flake.

Oxmoor Dikes

SE 894 866
Cat. No. 1996.3.9
Bequest: Dr. J. Weyman
25 flints, mostly grey with some brown pieces. Predominantly unretouched flakes and blades but includes an end scraper, a broken retouched tool and a core scraper. Some are probably Mesolithic.

Sherburn

Sherburn Wold and East Wold
SE 970-5 732-8
SE 979-82 746-8
Cat. No. 1996.3.4
Bequest: Dr. J. Weyman
A total of 15 flints from Sherburn Wold and 19 flints from East Wold, Sherburn, collected by fieldwalking from various findspots. The East Wold material comprises a variety of grey coloured flint including some patinated pieces. They are mostly flakes and blades, some of which have been retouched. Generally Late Mesolithic. The Sherburn Wold material includes two microlithic bladelets and a number of retouched flakes. This group includes light and dark grey flint. Late Mesolithic.

Sherburn, Eastwold
SE 97 74
Cat. No. 1996.3.13
Bequest: Dr. J. Weyman
A single grey broken flint blade.

Thikleby Wold

SE 953 675
Cat. No. 1996.3.9
Bequest: Dr. J. Weyman
6 grey flints including scrapers and bladelets. Possibly Mesolithic.

Urchin Hill

Urchin Hill
SE 933 700
SE 934-7 700-5
Cat. No. 1996.3.1
Bequest: Dr. J. Weyman
A total of 150 flints collected by fieldwalking from various findspots. Collection includes cores, retouched blades and flakes, microliths, scrapers and waste. Mostly light grey flint, also some red-brown and medium grey flint. Overall this is a Mesolithic assemblage though it could contain Early Neolithic material. This assemblage would benefit from a more detailed evaluation.

Urchin Hill
SE 93 70
Cat. No. 1996.3.11
Bequest: Dr. J. Weyman
1 grey flint multi-platform bladelet core, probably Mesolithic.

Whitby

Whitby Area
Cat. No. 1963.10
Donor: G.H. Sadler
A single flint arrowhead.

Yorkshire Wolds

Yorkshire Wolds Area
Cat. No. 1925.1.106
A fine collection of 217 flints including 20 retouched and trimmed blades, 4 microliths, 11 leaf-shaped arrowheads, 18 barbed and tanged and transverse arrowheads including an unusual double tanged piece, a plano-convex knife and a gun flint. In addition there are many cores, knives and dozens of scrapers, the latter of which are predominantly Mesolithic. The assemblage is mostly light grey flint. Some pieces are heavily patinated while others have none at all. Early Mesolithic-Early Bronze Age. This is an important collection that would benefit from a more detailed assessment.

Yorkshire Wolds Area
Cat. No. 1996.3.10
Bequest: Dr. J. Weyman
A collection of 65 flints including many grey and white pieces. These are mostly flakes and blades, some of which are retouched, 2 platform bladelet cores, scrapers, a broken retouched blade tool and 2 end scrapers. Mesolithic-Early Neolithic and possibly some Early Bronze Age. Some pieces have light patination.

Yorkshire Wolds Area
Cat. No. 1996.5.2
Bequest: Dr. J. Weyman
A large collection of 160 flints including 22 modern home-made pieces. There are also 8 nodules, 2 hammerstones and 7 modern Mexican arrowheads. No provenances are associated with the actual flints in these bags and so cannot be matched to the grid

references contained in the written records. These records include the following entries: SE 93 70 (31 flints), TA 01 73 (13 flints), SE 96 70 (6 flints), SE 93 70 (6 flints), TA 00 74 (4 flints), SE 97 74 (1 flint), SE 97 68 (2 flints), SE 97 73 (2 flints), SE 89 86 (1 flint), TA 04 79 (1 flint). The collection contains some excellent material including platform cores, scrapers, arrowheads, awls, retouched flakes and blades, some possible microliths and a gun flint. The material is nearly all grey flint and some can be dated to the Mesolithic-Early Neolithic, though some may be Bronze Age. This collection deserves further attention although the lack of direct provenancing is frustrating.

MISCELLANEOUS

Denmark

Cat. No. 1972.26.I
Donor: Mrs. W. Percy Hedley
Ground and polished flint axe head with fine cutting edge from Denmark. Rectangular section, tapers in thickness at both ends. Early Neolithic.

Denmark
Cat. No. 1956.104.A
Donor: Mrs. W. Percy Hedley
A remarkable collection of lithics including 32 fine stone axe-heads made from a variety of material, 6 battle axes, 6 stone chisels, a flint axe fragment and a miniature of a flint axe, 4 flint daggers, 2 splendid flint sickles, 2 flint bi-faces and 9 long blades. Palaeolithic, Neolithic and Early Bronze Age.

France

Dordogne
Cat. No. 1985.31
Donor: Mr. W. Dodd
A total of 28 lithics, mostly large flakes.

Ireland

County Antrim
Cat. No. 1972.19
Donor: Mrs. W. Percy Hedley
2 flint spear points, one triangular shaped and the other barbed and tanged. Late Neolithic-Early Bronze Age.

County Antrim
Cat. No. 1923.22
Refs: *PSAN* 4th ser. 1 (1925): 128
A leaf-shaped arrowhead. Early Neolithic date.

Carnstone
Cat. No. No. 1923.23
Refs: *PSAN* 4th ser. 1 (1925): 128
A barbed and tanged arrowhead. Late Neolithic-Early Bronze Age.

Ireland
Cat. No. 1960.42
Donor: Mr. B. Upton
2 chert blades believed by donor to have come from Ireland.

Ireland
Cat. No. 1972.21
Donor: Mrs. W. Percy Hedley
Two barbed and tanged arrowheads and a leaf-shaped arrowhead. Former Late Neolithic-Early Bronze Age, latter Early Neolithic. These finds probably come from Ireland.

Lakenheath

Lakenheath, Suffolk
Cat. No. 1972.8
Donor: Mrs. W. Percy Hedley
A flint hand-axe (Palaeolithic) and flint side scraper.

Milden Hall

Warren Hill, Milden Hall, Suffolk
Cat. No. 1972.7
Donor: Mrs. W. Percy Hedley
Assortment of 9 implements including flint axes, scrapers and other tools.

Milton Earnest

Hollow Farm, Milton Earnest, Bedfordshire
Cat. No. 1973.9
Donor: D.K. Hutton
Single Palaeolith

Scottish Borders

Various Locations
Cat. No. 2002.17
Donor: Robinson Library
Collection of flints comprised solely of scrapers with the exception of a fine group of 14 unprovenanced arrowheads. There are a variety of scraper forms present including side scrapers, hollow scrapers, end scrapers and thumbnail scrapers from various named locations. The scrapers are made from a mixture of glacial flint and, occasionally, nodular flint. There are 6 very fine barbed and tanged arrowheads and 9 leaf-shaped arrowheads mostly of honey-coloured flint. There are an additional 9 scrapers from unknown locations.

Coldstream, Wark Common
A single light grey flint scraper with abrupt retouch. Possibly Mesolithic

Denholm
5 small grey flint scrapers, some with abrupt retouch. Mesolithic -Bronze Age.

Earlston

21 scrapers including side scrapers and thumbnails. Made from grey, brown and white flint. Mesolithic-Bronze Age.

Fairmington

2 scrapers with abrupt retouch made from grey flint. Possibly Neolithic.

Haliburton, Greenlaw

9 small scrapers, mostly thumbnails, made from grey and orange flint. Some have abrupt retouch while others have shallow retouch. Mesolithic- Bronze Age.

Jedburgh, Shaps Law

1 tiny scraper with abrupt retouch made from grey flint. Possibly Mesolithic.

Kelso, Hoselaw

11 small scrapers made on grey, white and brown flint. Some have abrupt retouch. Mesolithic – Bronze Age.

Lauder, Border House

3 scrapers made from grey flint and one from chert. Probably Neolithic – Bronze Age.

Melrose

A single tiny scraper with abrupt retouch made from grey flint. Possibly Mesolithic.

Unknown

12 scrapers, mostly thumbnails, of light grey flint with 3 dark grey, 1 fawn and 1 red-brown and light light grey. Neolithic – Bronze Age.

Unknown

9 leaf-shaped arrowheads and 6 barbed and tanged arrowheads made from honey coloured, red-brown and light grey flint. Early Neolithic – Early Bronze Age.

Seaford

Seaford, Sussex
Cat. No. 1972.14
Donor: Mrs. W. Percy Hedley
A single grey flint implement of oval shape with one edge sharpened and another roughly squared off. Donor suggested it was for use as a plane.

Southall Gas Works

Southhall Gas Works Site
Cat. No. 1972.13
Donor: Mrs. W. Percy Hedley
A flint axe head found whilst gas works under construction.

Sturry

Sturry, Kent
Cat. No. 1972.17
Donor: Mrs. W. Percy Hedley
2 Palaeolithic hand-axes including an ovate (Acheulian) that is heavily patinated, though chipped area shows it is made from grey flint.

Tripolitania

Zella, Tripolitania
Cat. No. 1967.6
Donor: Sunderland Museum and Art Gallery
Collection of 354 flint artefacts found c.1966. Mesolithic-Neolithic. Many finished tools made on medium grey flint with occasional honey-coloured flint. Many microliths, arrowheads and scrapers. Also includes a collection of 15 fine, large blade tools.

Unknown

Cat. No. 1925.1.108
Donor: T. Stephens
Collection of 5 large flints. Includes 2 gun flints and 2 large broad blades of the same dark grey matt material. There is also a small flaked flint axe miniature.

Cat. No. 1956.50
Massive single platform, dark brown patinated flint core. Likely to have come from abroad. A large ground axe head made of coarse-grained igneous rock, also likely to be from abroad.

Cat. No. 1956.105.A
Medium grey flint spear point with slight tang. Probably an import from America.

Cat. No. 1972.11
Donor: Mrs. W. Percy Hedley
A dark grey flint chipped into a globular shape.

Cat. No. 1956.264.A
A large light grey flint spear point retouched along the longest edge.

Cat. No. 1956.27.A
Collection of 5 lithics including 4 bifacially worked flakes, one of which could be part of a stone axe head and another a scraper, the other 2 being small ovates that could feasibly be Palaeolithic, but their fresh appearance and small size suggests they are later. There are also 6 stone axes, or fragments thereof, one of which is made from flint.

Cat. No. 1972.15
Donor: Mrs. W. Percy Hedley
Collection of 5 leaf-shaped flint implements, 4 of which are probably small hand axes and utilised flakes; the fifth piece is a smaller retouched flake. 3 of the pieces are patinated. They are

made of a variety of grey flints and are likely to be Palaeolithic, probably Acheulian.

Cat. No. 1972.10
Donor: Mrs. W. Percy Hedley
Collection of 10 flint tools including blades and fabricators. All are made from grey flint with 3 patinated white. Probably Mesolithic – Neolithic.

Cat. No. 1972.12
Donor: Mrs. W. Percy Hedley
Flint pounding stone.

Cat. No. 1972.16
Donor: Mrs. W. Percy Hedley
Collection of 3 ovate flake flint implements, probably Acheulian. All are patinated though it is evident that two are made from a grey flint.

Cat. No. 1972.20
Donor: Mrs. W. Percy Hedley
A single flint retouched blade tool, possibly a variant of a plano-convex knife. Although made of grey flint it is very heavily patinated. Possibly Early Bronze Age.

Cat. No. 1978.7
Donor: Mr. H. Hornsby
A light grey flint flake struck from a previously chipped patinated piece.

Cat. No. 1972.26.II
Donor: Mrs. W. Percy Hedley
A single fine ground and polished flint axe head. Rechipping of the axe indicates it was rejuvenated for flint production. Straight-sided with rectangular section. Early Neolithic.

Cat. No. 1996.8
Bequest: Dr. J. Weyman
There are various pieces in the 1996.8 collection that have no stated provenance although it is highly likely that they come from north Northumberland in the Milfield area. There are 23 flakes and chips, of agate, flint and chert and are in a variety of colours including mostly reds and greys. None of the pieces are diagnostic.

Cat. No. 1960.3.A
Donor: Mr. C.M. Daniels
Ref: Manning 1976.
5 small flint/chert arrowheads made from a grey material probably from North Africa. All are tanged and similar from the material from Tripolitania.

Cat. No. 1978.16
Collection of 9 flints including 2 good examples of gun flints, a fine oblique arrowhead with broken tang, an oblique arrowhead with broken tip, an edge-trimmed blade, a rejuvenation flake, a broken invasively retouched flake, 2 flakes and a fragment of mudstone.

Cat. No. 1985.32
Collection of 19 flints of various colours, some patinated. Mostly flakes but also cores, a core rejuvenation flake and a broken blade segment.

Wallingford

Wallingford, Berkshire
Cat. No. 1972.18
Donor: Mrs. W. Percy Hedley
A bi-facial hand-axe made from a brown flint. Probably Acheulian.

Bibliography and Further Reading

Addington, L. R. 1986. *Lithic Illustration: Drawing Flaked Stone Artifacts for Publication.* Chicago and London: University of Chicago Press.

Affleck, T. L., Edwards, K. and Clarke, A. 1988. Archaeological and palynological studies at the Mesolithic pitchstone and flint site at Auchareoch, Isle of Arran. *Proceedings of the Society of Antiquaries of Scotland* 118: 37-59.

Anderson, P. C. 1980. A testimony of prehistoric tasks: diagnostic residues on stone tool working edges. *World Archaeology* 12(2): 181-194.

Andrefsky, W. 1998. *Lithics. Macroscopic Approaches to Analysis.* Cambridge: Cambridge University Press.

Annable, R. 1987. *The Later Prehistory of Northern England. Cumbria, Northumberland and Durham from the Neolithic to the Late Bronze Age.* Oxford: British Archaeological Reports, British Series 160.

Arora, S. K. 1973. Mittelsteinzeilliche formengruppen zwischen Rhein und Weser. In S. K. Kozlowski (ed.) *The Mesolithic in Europe.* Warsaw: Warsaw University Press: 9-22.

Ashton, N. and David, A. (eds.) 1994. *Stories in Stone.* London: Lithic Studies Society.

Ashton, N., Healy, F. and Pettitt, P. (eds.) 1998. *Stone Age Archaeology: Essays in honour of John Wymer.* Oxford: Oxbow Monograph 102/Lithic Studies Society Occasional Paper 6.

Barber, M., Field, D. and Topping, P. 1999. *The Neolithic flint mines of England.* Swindon: English Heritage.

Barton, R. N. E. 1992. *Hengistbury Head Dorset.* Oxford: Oxford University Committee for Archaeology Monograph No. 4.

Barton, R. N. E. 1997. *Stone Age Britain.* London: B.T. Batsford and English Heritage.

Barton, N., Roberts, A.J. and Roe, D.A. 1991. *The Late Glacial in North-west Europe: Human Adaptation and Environmental Change at the End of the Pleistocene.* London: CBA Research Report No. 77.

Blankholm, H. P. 1985. Maglemosekulturens hyttegrundrids. En undersøgelser af bebyggelse og adfærdsmønstre i tidlig mesolitisk tid. *Aarbøger for Nordisk Oldkyndighed og Historie* 1984: 61 - 77.

Blankholm, H. P. 1993. Barmose I Revisited. *Mesolithic Miscellany* 14(1 & 2): 12 - 14.

Bonsall, C., (ed.) 1989. *The Mesolithic in Europe.* Edinburgh: John Donald.

Bordaz, J. 1971. *Tools of the Old and New Stone Age.* Newton Abbot: David and Charles.

Bradley, R. 1978. *The Prehistoric Settlement of Britain.* London: Routledge & Kegan Paul.

Bradley, R. 1987. Flint Technology and the Character of Neolithic Settlement. In A. G. Brown and M. R. Edmonds (eds.) *Lithic Analysis and Later British Prehistory. Some Problems and Approaches.* Oxford: British Archaeological Reports, British Series 162: 181-185.

Bradley, R. 1995. Fieldwalking without flints: worked quartz as a clue to the character of prehistoric settlement. *Oxford Journal of Archaeology* 14 (1): 13-22.

Bradley, R. 1998. *The Significance of Monuments. On the Shaping of Human Experience in Neolithic and Bronze Age Europe.* London: Routeledge.

Bradley, R. and Edmonds, M.R. 1993. *Interpreting the axe trade.* Cambridge: Cambridge University Press.

Brézillon, M. 1983. *La Denomination des Objets de Pierre Taillée.* Paris, CNRS.

Brooks, I. and Phillips, P. (eds.) 1989. *Breaking the Stony Silence. Papers from the Sheffield Lithics Conference 1988.* Oxford: British Archaeological Reports, British Series 213.

Brown, A. G. and Edmonds, M.R. (eds.) 1987. *Lithic Analysis and Later British Prehistory. Some Problems and Approaches.* Reading Studies in Archaeology No.2. Oxford, British Archaeological Reports, British Series 162.

Buckley, F. 1922. Early Tardenois remains at Bamburgh etc. *Proceedings of the Society of Antiquaries of Newcastle upon Tyne* 3rd ser, 10: 319-23.

Buckley, F. 1925. The microlithic industries of Northumberland. *Archaeologia Aeliana* 4th ser, 1: 42-7.

Burgess, C.B. 1972. Goatscrag, A Bronze Age rock shelter cemetery in North Northumberland. *Archaeologia Aeliana* 4th ser, 50: 15-69.

Burgess, C.B. 1984. The Prehistoric Settlement of Northumberland: A Speculative Survey. In R. Miket and C. Burgess (eds.) *Between And Beyond The Walls: Essays on the Prehistory and History of North Britain in Honour of George Jobey.* Edinburgh: John Donald: 126-175.

Burton, J. 1980. Making Sense of Waste Flakes: New Methods for Investigating the Technology and Economics Behind Chipped Stone Assemblages. *Journal of Archaeological Science* 7: 131-148.

Callahan, E. 1985. Experiments with Danish Mesolithic Microblade Technology. *Journal of Danish Archaeology* 4: 23-39.

Campbell, J. B. 1977. *The Upper Palaeolithic of Britain.* Vols I and II Oxford: Clarendon Press.

Clark, J.G.D. 1929. Discoidal polished flint knives – their typology and distribution. *Proceedings of the Prehistoric Society of East Anglia* 6(1): 40-54.

Clark, J.G.D. 1932. The Date of the Plano-Convex Flint-Knife in England and Wales. *Antiquaries Journal* 12: 158-162.

Clark, J.G.D. 1934a. Derivative Forms of the Petit Tranchet in Britain. *Archaeological Journal* 91: 34-58.

Clark, J.G.D. 1934b. The classification of a microlithic culture: the Tardenoisian of Horsham. *Archaeological Journal* 90: 52-77.

Clark, J.G.D. 1946. Seal hunting in the stone age of north-western Europe: a study in economic prehistory. *Proceedings of the Prehistoric Society* 12: 12-48.

Clark, J.G.D. 1954. *Excavations at Star Carr. An Early Mesolithic site at Seamer near Scarborough, Yorkshire.* Cambridge: Cambridge University Press.

Clark, J.G.D. 1955. A microlithic industry from the Cambridgeshire Fenland and other industries of Sauveterrian affinities from Britain. *Proceedings of the Prehistoric Society* 21: 3-20.

Clark, J.G.D. 1958. Blade and trapeze industries of the European stone age. *Proceedings of the Prehistoric Society* 24: 24-42.

Clark, J.G.D. 1960. *The Stone Age Hunters.* London. Thames and Hudson.

Clark, J.G.D. 1967. Excavations at the Neolithic site at Hurst Fen, Mildenhall, Suffolk, 1954, 1957 and 1958. *Proceedings of the Prehistoric Society* 26: 202-45.

Clark, J.G.D. and Godwin, H. 1956. A Maglemosian Site at Brandesburton, Holderness, Yorkshire. *Proceedings of the Prehistoric Society* 22: 6 - 22.

Clark, J.G.D. and Rankine, W.F. 1939. Excavations at Farnham, Surrey (1937-38): the Horsham culture and the question of Mesolithic dwellings. *Proceedings of the Prehistoric Society* 5: 61-118.

Clarke, D. V., Cowie, T.G. and Foxon, A. 1985. *Symbols of Power at the Time of Stonehenge.* Edinburgh: National Museum of Antiquities of Scotland and H.M.S.O.

Clarke, J.G.D. and Fell, C.I. 1953. Early Iron Age site at Micklemoor Hill, West Harling, Norfolk. *Proceedings of the Prehistoric Society* 19: 1-40.

Clough, T.H.M. and Cummins, W.A. (eds.) 1979. *Stone Axe Studies. Archaeological, Petrological, Experimental and Ethnographic.* London: CBA Research Report 23.

Clough, T.H.M. and Cummins, W.A. (eds.) 1988. *Stone Axe Studies. The Petrology of Prehistoric Stone Implements from the British Isles.* London: CBA Research Report 67.

Coles, J.M. 1971. The early settlement of Scotland: excavations at Morton, Fife. *Proceedings of the Prehistoric Society* 37: 284-366.

Coles, J.M. 1983. Morton Revisited. In A. O'Connor and D.V. Clarke (eds.). *From the Stone-Age to the Forty-Five.* Edinburgh: John Donald: 9-18.

Coles, B. 1998. Doggerland: A speculative survey. *Proceedings of the Prehistoric Society* 64: 45-81.

Cooney, G. 1998. Breaking stones, making places: the social landscape of axe production sites. In A. Gibson and D. Simpson (eds.) *Prehistoric Ritual and Religion.* Stroud: Sutton Publishing Ltd: 108-118.

Cooney, G. and Mandal, S. 1998. *The Irish Stone-Axe Project.* Bray: Wordwell Ltd.

Crabtree, D. 1968. Mesoamerican Polyhedral Cores and Prismatic Blades. *American Antiquity* 33(4): 446-478.

Cummins, W. and Harding, A. 1988. *The Petrological Identification of Stone Implements From North-East England. Stone Axe Studies Volume 2.* Clough and Cummins. London: Council for British Archaeology: 78-84.

Curwen, E. and Curwen, E.C. 1926. Harrow Hill Flint Mine Excavation, 1924-5. *Sussex Archaeological Collections* 67: 103-38.

Darbishire, R.D. 1874. Notes on discoveries in Ehenside Tarn. *Archaeologia* 44: 273-92.

Dumont, J. V. 1987. Mesolithic microwear research in Northwest Europe. In P. Rowley-Conwy, M. Zvelebil and H. P. Blinkholm (eds.) *Mesolithic Northwest Europe: Recent Trends.* Sheffield: University of Sheffield: 82-89.

Dumont, J. V. 1988. *A Microwear Analysis of Selected Artefact Types from the Mesolithic Sites of Star Carr and Mount Sandal.* Oxford: British Archaeological Reports, British Series 187.

Edmonds, M.R. 1992. 'Their use is wholly unknown'. In N. Sharples and A. Sheridan (eds.) *Vessels for the Ancestors. Essays on the Neolithic of Britain and Ireland.* Edinburgh: Edinburgh University Press: 179-193.

Edmonds, M.R. 1995. *Stone Tools And Society. Working Stone in Neolithic and Bronze Age Britain.* London: B.T. Batsford.

Eliade, M. 1978. *The Forge and the Crucible: The Origins and Structures of Alchemy.* Chicago: University of Chicago Press.

Ellis, C.J. and Lothrop, J.C. (eds) 1989. *Eastern Paleoindian Lithic Resource Use.* (Westview Investigations in American Archaeology). Boulder: Westview Press.

Ericson, J. E. and Purdy, B.A. (eds.) 1984. *Prehistoric Quarries and Lithic Production.* New Directions in Archaeology. London: Cambridge University Press.

Eriksen, B.V. 2000. *Flintsudies. En håndbog i Systematiske Analyser af Flintinventarer.* Aarhus: Universitetsforlag Aarhus.

Evens, E. D., Grinsell, L.V., Piggott, S. and Wallis, F.S. 1962. Fourth report of the sub-committee of the South-Western group of Museums and Art Galleries (England) on the petrological identification of stone axes. *Proceedings of the Prehistoric Society* 28: 209-66.

Fasham, P.J. and Ross, J.M. 1978. A Bronze Age flint industry from a barrow site in Micheldever Wood, Hampshire. *Proceedings of the Prehistoric Society* 14: 47-67.

Finlayson, B. 1990. Lithic exploitation during the Mesolithic in Scotland. *Scottish Archaeological Review* 7: 41-57.

Fischer, A., Vemming Hansen, P. and Rasmussen, P. 1984. Macro and Micro Wear Traces on Lithic Projectile Points. Experimental Results and Prehistoric Examples. *Journal of Danish Archaeology* 3: 19-46.

Ford, S., Bradley, R., Hawkes, J. and Fisher, P. 1984. Flint-working in the age of metal. *Oxford Journal of Archaeology* 3: 157-73.

Gamble, C. 1986. *The Palaeolithic Settlement of Europe.* Cambridge: Cambridge University Press.

Garrod, D. 1926. *The Upper Palaeolithic Age in Britain.* Oxford: Clarendon Press.

Gendel, P.A. 1984. *Mesolithic Social Territories in Northwestern Europe.* Oxford: British Archaeological Reports International Series 218.

Gero, J. M. 1989. Assessing social information in material objects: how well do lithics measure up? In R. Torrence (ed.) *Time, Energy and Stone Tools.* Cambridge: Cambridge University Press: 92-105.

Grace, R. 1989. *Interpreting the Function of Stone Tools.* Oxford: British Archaeological Reports, International Series 474.

Green, S. 1980. *The Flint Arrowheads of the British Isles.* Oxford: British Archaeological Reports, British Series 75

Griffiths, D. R., Bergman, C.A., Clayton, C.J., Ohnuma, K., Robins, G.V. and Seeley, N.J. 1987. Experimental investigation of the heat treatment of flint. In G. de G. Sieveking and M.M. Newcomer (eds.). *The Human Uses of Flint and Chert.* Cambridge: Cambridge University Press: 43-52.

Griffiths, N., Jenner, A. and Wilson, C. 1990. *Drawing Archaeological Finds. A Manual.* Occasional Paper No.13 of the Institute of Archaeology, UCL. London: Archetype Publications Ltd.

Grimes, W.F. 1932. The Early Bronze Age flint dagger in England and Wales. *Proceedings of the Prehistoric Society of East Anglia* 6 (4): 340-55.

Grøn, O. 1987. Reconstruction of Social Structure of the Maglemose Culture of Southern Scandinavia and Northern Germany. *Mesolithic Miscellany* 8(1): 18-19.

Grøn, O. 1989. General Spatial Behaviour in Small Dwellings: A Preliminary Study in Ethnoarchaeology and Social Psychology. In C. J. Bonsall (ed.) *The Mesolithic in Europe: Papers Presented at the Third International Symposium, Edinburgh 1985.* Edinburgh: John Donald Publishers Limited: 99 - 105.

Grøn, O. 1995. *The Maglemose Culture: The Reconstruction of the Social Organization of a Mesolithic Culture in Northern Europe.* Oxford: Tempus Reparatum.

Harding, A. 1981. Excavations in the prehistoric ritual complex near Milfield, Northumberland. *Proceedings of the Prehistoric Society* 46: 87-135.

Harding, D. W. 1970. County Durham in the Prehistoric Period. *Transactions of the Architectural and Archaeological Society of Northumberland and Durham* 2: 27-30.

Harper, K. 1937. Acheulian flake tools. *Proceedings of the Prehistoric Society* 3: 15-28.

Haselgrove, C. C., Ferrel, G. and Turnbull, P. 1988. *The Durham Archaeological Survey 1983-87.* Durham, Department of Archaeology, University of Durham.

Haselgrove, C. C. and Healey, F. 1992. The Prehistory of the Tyne-Tees Lowlands: Some Recent Finds. *Durham Archaeological Journal* 8: 1-24.

Healy, F. 1984. Lithic Assemblage Variation in the Late Third and Early Second Millennia BC in Eastern England. *Lithics* 5: 10-18.

Hoard, R.C., Holen, S.R., Glascock, M.D., Neff, H. and Elam, J.M. 1992. Neutron Activation Analysis of stone from the Chadron formation and a Clovis site on the Great Plains. *Journal of Archaeological Science* 19: 655-665.

Hodder, I. 1982. *Symbols in Action: Ethnoarchaeological Studies of Material Culture.* Cambridge: Cambridge University Press.

Holgate, R. 1991. *Prehistoric Flint Mines.* Princes Risborough: Shire.

Hubert, F. 1988. L'exploitation du silex à Spiennes. *Archaeologicum Belgii Speculum* XV.

Hubert, F. 1990. Essai de restitution de la technique de foudroyage du silex dans une minière néolithique de Spiennes. In Séronie-Vivien, M.-R., & M. Lenoir (eds.) *Le Silex de sa Genèse à L'outil. Actes du V° Colloque International sur le Silex. (Vth International Flint Symposium), Bordeaux, 17 sept.-2 oct. 1987.* Cahiers du Quaternaire 17. Bordeaux, CNRS: 1-310 (volume I), 311-645 (volume II).

Humphrey, J. and Young, R. 1999. Flint use in Later Bronze Age and Iron Age England - still a fiction? *Lithics* 20: 57-61.

Inizan, M.-L., Reduron-Ballinger, M., Roche, H. and Tixier, J. 1999. *Technology and Terminology of Knapped Stone.* Nanterre: CREP.

Jacobi, R.M. 1976. Britain inside and outside Mesolithic Europe. *Proceedings of the Prehistoric Society* 42: 67-84.

Jacobi, R.M. 1978. Northern England in the eighth millenium bc: an essay. In Mellars, P.A. (ed.) *The Early Postglacial Settlement of Northern Europe.* London: Duckworth, 295-332.

Jacobi, R. M. 1979. Early Flandrian hunters in the South-West. *Proceedings of the Devon Archaeological Society* 37: 48-93.

Jacobi, R. M. 1986. The Lateglacial archaeology of Gough's Cave at Cheddar. In S. N. Collcutt. (ed.) *The Palaeolithic of Britain and its Nearest Neighbours: Recent Trends.* Sheffield: Department of Archaeology and Prehistory, University of Sheffield: 75-9.

Jarvis, H.W. 1995. INAA characteristics of Onondaga Chert: A preliminary study in Western New York. *Northeastern Anthropological Association 29th Annual Meeting.* University of Montreal: 15-19.

Jenkinson, R. D. S. 1984. *Creswell Crags.* Oxford: British Archaeological Reports, British Series 122.

Jobey, I. and Jobey, G. 1988. Gowanburn river camp: an Iron Age, Romano-British and more recent settlement in North Tynedale, Northumberland. *Archaeologia Aeliana* 5th ser 16: 11-28.

Johnson, L. L. 1978. A History of Flint-knapping Experimentation, 1838-1976. *Current Anthropology* 19: 337-372.

Jørgansen, S. 1985. *Tree-Felling in Draved.* Copenhagen: National Museum of Denmark.

Justice, N.D. 1989. Prehistoric quarries and workshops: The Wyandotte chert source and the evidence for manufacture, trade, and ritual behavior. *Current Research in Indiana Archaeology and Prehistory: 1987.* Glenn A. Black Laboratory of Archaeology, Research Reports No. 10.

Keen, L. and Radley, J. 1971. Report on the petrological identification of stone axes from Yorkshire. *Proceedings of the Prehistoric Society* 37: 16-37.

Kelley, H. 1937. Acheulian flake tools. *Proceedings of the Prehistoric Society* 3: 15-28.

Kempe, D.R.C. and Templeman, J.A. 1983. The petrology of archaeological artefacts. In D.R.C. Kempe and A.P. Harvey (eds.) *Techniques in the Petrology of Archaeological Artefacts:* 26-52. Oxford, Clarendon Press.

Lacaille, A.D. 1954. *The Stone Age in Scotland.* Oxford, Oxford University Press.

Longworth, I and Varndell, G. 1996 *Excavations at Grimes Graves, Norfolk 1972-76. Fasicule 5 Mining in the Deeper Mines.* London: British Musuem Press.

Lord, J.W. 1993. *The Nature and Subsequent Uses of Flint Volume 1. The Basics of Lithic Technology.* John Lord.

Luedtke, B.E. 1992. *An Archaeologist's Guide to Chert and Flint.* Los Angeles: UCLA, Institute of Archaeology.

Mallouf, R.J. 1982. An analysis of plow-damaged chert artifacts: the Brookeen Creek Cache (41H186), Hill County, Texas. *Journal of Field Archaeology* 9: 79-98.

Mandeville, M.D. 1973. A consideration of the thermal pretreatment of chert. *Plains Anthropology* 18: 177-202.

Manning, W.H. 1976. *Catalogue of Romano-British Ironwork in the Museum of Antiquities, Newcastle upon Tyne.* Newcastle upon Tyne.

Marshall, D. 1977. Carved stone balls. *Proceedings of the Society of Antiquaries of Scotland* 108: 40-72.

Marshall, D.N. 1983. Further notes on carved stone balls. *Proceedings of the Society of Antiquaries of Scotland* 113: 628-30.

Martingell, H. 1988. The flint industry. In T. J. Wilkinson (ed.) *Archaeology and Environment in South Essex:* 70-73.

Martingell, H. and Saville, A. 1988. *The Illustration of Lithic Artefacts: A Guide to Drawing Stone Tools for Specialist Reports.* Northampton: Lithic Studies Society Occasional Paper No. 3 and Association of Archaeological Illustrators and Surveyors Technical Paper No. 9.

Masters, L. 1984. The Neolithic Long Cairns of Cumbria and Northumberland. In R. Miket and C. Burgess (eds.) *Between And Beyond The Walls: Essays in Honour of George Jobey.* Edinburgh: John Donald: 52-73.

Mellars, P. 1970. An antler harpoon-head of 'Obanian' affinities from Whitburn, County Durham. *Archaeologia Aeliana* 4th ser. 48: 337-46.

Mellars, P. 1996. *The Neanderthal Legacy. An Archaeological Perspective from Western Europe.* Princeton, New Jersey: Princeton University Press

Mellars, P.A. and Stringer, C. (eds.)1989. *The Human Revolution: Behavioural and Biological Perspectives on the Origins of Modern Humans.* Edinburgh: Edinburgh University Press.

Mercer, R.J. 1980. *Hambledon Hill. A Neolithic Landscape.* Edinburgh: Edinburgh University Press.

Mercer, R. 1981a. Excavations at Carn Brea, a Neolithic fortified complex of the third millennium BC. *Cornish Archaeology* 25: 1-204.

Mercer, R. 1981b. *Grimes Graves, Norfolk. Excavations 1971-72.* London: H.M.S.O.

Miket, R. 1984. *The Prehistory of Tyne and Wear.* Newcastle upon Tyne: Northumberland Archaeological Group.

Miket, R. 1985. Ritual Enclosures at Whitton Hill, Northumberland. *Proceedings of the Prehistoric Society* 51: 137-148.

Miket, R. 1987. *The Milfield Basin, Northumberland 4000 BC - AD 800.* Unpublished Mlitt. Thesis, University of Newcastle Upon Tyne.

Morrison, A. 1980. *Early Man in Britain and Ireland.* London: Croom Helm Ltd.

Mulholland, H. 1970. The microlithic industries of the Tweed valley. *Transactions of the Dumfriesshire and Galloway Natural History and Antiquarian Society* 3rd ser, 47: 81-110.

Myers, A. 1989. Reliable and maintainable technological strategies in the Mesolithic of mainland Britain. In R. Torrence (ed.) *Time, Energy and Stone Tools.* Cambridge: Cambridge University Press: 78-91.

Myers, A.M. 1987. All shot to pieces? Inter-assemblage variability, lithic analysis and Mesolithic assemblage 'types'; some preliminary observations. In A. G. Brown and M. R. Edmonds (eds.) *Lithic Analysis and Later British Prehistory. Some Problems and Approaches.* Oxford: British Archaeological Reports, British Series 162: 137-153.

Newcomer, M.H. and Karlin, C. 1987. Flint chips from Pincevent. In G. de G. Sieveking and M. H. Newcomer (eds.) *The Human Uses of Flint and Chert.* Cambridge: Cambridge University Press: 33-7.

Newcomer, M.H., Grace, R. and Unga-Hamilton, R. 1987. Microwear polishes, blind tests and texture. In G. de G. Sieveking and M. H. Newcomer (eds.) *The Human Uses of Flint and Chert.* Cambridge: Cambridge University Press: 253-263.

Newell, R.R. 1973. The Post-Glacial Adaptations of the Indigenous Population of the Northwest European Plain. In S. K. Kozlowski. (ed.) *The Mesolithic in Europe: Papers read at the International Archaeological Symposium on the Mesolithic in Europe, Warsaw, May, 7 - 12, 1973.* Warsaw: Warsaw University Press: 399 - 440.

Olausson, D.S. 1983. Experiments to investigate the effects of heat treatment on use-wear on flint tools. *Proceedings of the Prehistoric Society* 49: 1-13.

Patterson, L.W. and Sollberger, J.B. 1979. Water treatment of flint. *Lithic Technology* 8(3): 50-51.

Pitts, M.W. 1978. On the shape of waste flakes as an index of technological change in lithic industries. *Journal of Archaeological Science* 5: 17-37.

Pitts, M. 1996. The stone axe in Neolithic Britain. *Proceedings of the Prehistoric Society* 62: 311-371.

Pitts, M.W. and Jacobi, R.M. 1979. Some Aspects of Change in Flaked Stone Industries of the Mesolithic and Neolithic in Southern England. *Journal of Archaeological Science* 6: 163-177.

Preston, H. 1929. Flintwork sites in NE Durham. *Vasculum* 15: 137-141.

Price, T.D., Chappell, S. and Ives, D.J. 1982. Thermal alteration in Mesolithic assemblages. *Proceedings of the Prehistoric Society* 48: 467-485.

Pull, J.H. 1932. *The Flintminers of Blackpatch.* London: Williams and Norgate.

Radley, J. and Mellars, P. 1964. A Mesolithic structure at Deepcar, Yorkshire, England and the affinities of its associated flint industries. *Proceedings of the Prehistoric Society* 30: 1-24.

Radley, J., Tallis, J.H. and Switsur, V.R. 1974. The excavation of three 'narrow blade' Mesolithic sites in the southern Pennines, England. *Proceedings of the Prehistoric Society* 40: 1-19.

Rapp, G. and Hill, C.L. 1998. *Geoarchaeology: The Earth Science Approach to Archaeological Interpretation.* Yale University Press.

Reynier, M.J. 1998. Early Mesolithic settlement in England and Wales: some preliminary observations. In N. Ashton, F. Healy, and P. Pettitt (eds.) *Stone Age Archaeology: Essays in Honour of John Wymer.* Oxford: Oxbow Monograph 102/Lithic Studies Society Occasional Paper 6: 174-184.

Robertson-Mackay, R. 1987. Excavations at Staines, Middlesex. *Proceedings of the Prehistoric Society* 63: 1-47.

Robins, P. 1996. Worked flint. In T. Ashwin (ed.) Excavation of an Iron Age site at Silfield, Wymondham, Norfolk, 1992-93. *Norfolk Archaeology* 42 (3): 266-270.

Roe, D.A. 1968a. British Lower and Middle Palaeolithic handaxe groups. *Proceedings of the Prehistoric Society* 34: 1-82.

Roe, D. 1968b. *A Gazetteer of British Lower and Middle Palaeolithic sites.* London: CBA Research Report, 8.

Roe, D.A. 1981. *The Lower and Middle Palaeolithic Periods in Britain.* London: Routledge & Kegan Paul.

Roe, F.E.S. 1966. The battle-axe series in Britain. *Proceedings of the Prehistoric Society* 32: 199-245.

Rosen, S.A. 1997. *Lithics after the Stone Age.* Walnut Creek: Altamira Press.

Russell, M. 2001. *Rough Quarries, Rocks and Hills. John Pull and the Flint Mines of Sussex.* Bournemouth School of Conservation Sciences Occasional Paper 6. Oxford: Oxbow Books.

Saville, A. 1977. Two Mesolithic implement types. *Northamptonshire Archaeology* 12: 3-8.

Saville, A. 1980. On the measurement of struck flakes and flake tools. *Lithics* 1: 16-20.

Saville, A. 1981a. *Grimes Graves, Norfolk, Excavations 1971-72: Vol. II, The Flint Assemblage.* London: HMSO. Department of the Environment Archaeological Report 11.

Saville, A. 1981b. Iron Age flint working - fact or fiction? *Lithics* 2: 6-9.

Saville, A. 1990. *Hazleton North, Gloucestershire, 1979-82: The Excavation of a Neolithic Long Cairn of the Cotswold-Severn group.* London: English Heritage.

Saville, A. 1994. Exploitation of lithic resources for stone tools in earlier prehistoric Scotland. In N. Ashton and A. David (eds.) *Stories in Stone.* London: Lithic Studies Society Occasional Paper No. 4: 57-70.

Saville, A. 1995. Prehistoric exploitation of flint from the Buchan Ridge Gravels, Grampian Region, north-east Scotland. *Archaeologia Polona* 33: 353-68.

Saville, A. 1997. Palaeolithic handaxes in Scotland. *Proceedings of the Society of Antiquaries of Scotland* 127: 1-16.

Saville, A. 1998. Studying the Mesolithic period in Scotland: A bibliographic gazetteer. In N. Ashton, F. Healy, and P. Pettitt (eds.) 1998. *Stone Age Archaeology: Essays in honour of John Wymer.* Oxford: Oxbow Monograph 102/Lithic Studies Society Occasional Paper 6: 211-224.

Saville, A. 2001. A Mesolithic barbed antler point from the foreshore of the Forth Estuary, near Carriden, Falkirk. *Calatria* 15: 70-80.

Saville, A. 2002. Lithic artefacts from Neolithic causewayed enclosures: character and meaning. In G. Varndell and P. Topping (eds), *Enclosures in Neolithic Europe.* Oxford: Oxbow Books, 91-105.

Saville, A. and Ballin, T.B. 2000. Quartz technology in Scottish Prehistory. *Lithics* 21: 45-51.

Schild, R. and Sulgostowska, Z. (eds.) 1997. *Man and Flint.* Warszawa: Institute of Archaeology and Ethnography.

Schmalz, R.F. 1960. Flint and the patination of flint artefacts. *Proceedings of the Prehistoric Society* 26: 44-49.

Schofield, A.J. (ed.) 1995. *Lithics in Context.* London: Lithic Studies Society.

Sheets, P. D. 1987. Dawn of a new Stone Age in eye surgery. In R. J. Sharer and W. Ashmore. (eds.) *Archaeology. Discovering Our Past.* Mountain View, California: Mayfield Publishing Company: 230-31.

Shepherd, W. 1972. *Flint. Its Origin, Properties and Uses.* London: Faber.

Simmons, I. G. 1996. *The Environmental Impact of Later Mesolithic Cultures.* Edinburgh: Edinburgh University Press.

Simpson, D. D. A. 1996. 'Crown' antler maceheads and the later Neolithic in Britain. *Proceedings of the Prehistoric Society* 62: 293-309.

Singer, R., Wymer, J.J., Gladfelter, B.G. and Wolff, R.G. 1973. Clacton-on-Sea, Essex: report on excavations 1969-70. *Proceedings of the Prehistoric Society* 39: 6-74.

Smith, C. 1992. *Late Stone Age Hunters of the British Isles.* London: Routledge.

Smith, I.F. 1965. *Windmill Hill and Avebury: Excavations by Alexander Keiller 1925-39.* Oxford: Clarendon Press.

Sockett, E. 1971. Stone axes from Heddon-on-the-Wall. *Archaeologia Aeliana* 4th ser. 49: 240-4.

Speak, S. and Aylett, M. 1996. The Carved Stone Ball from Hetton, Northumberland. *Northern Archaeology* (Special Edition) 13/14: 179-181.

Stafford, M. 1998. In Search of Hindsgavl: Experiments in the Production of Neolithic Danish Flint Daggers. *Antiquity* 72 (276): 187 – 212.

Stafford, M. 1999. *From Forager to Farmer in Flint: A Lithic Analysis of the Prehistoric Transition to Agriculture in Southern Scandinavia.* Århus: Aarhus University Press.

Stone, J. F. S. 1932. Easton Down, Winterslow, South Wiltshire, Flint Mine Excavation, 1930. *Wiltshire Archaeological and Natural History Magazine* 45: 350-65.

Stringer, C.B. 1993. *In Search of the Neanderthals: Solving the Puzzle of Human Origins*. New York: Thames and Hudson.

Stringer, C.B. 1996. The Boxgrove tibia: Britain's oldest hominid and its place in the Middle Pleistocene record. In C. Gamble and A. J. Lawson. (eds.) *The English Palaeolithic Reviewed*. Salisbury: Wessex Archaeology: 52-6.

Stuart, A.J. 1988. *Life in the Ice Age*. Princes Risborough: Shire.

Taçon, P.S.C. 1991. The power of stone: symbolic aspects of stone use and tool development in western Arnhem Land, Australia. *Antiquity* 65: 192-207.

Tait, J. 1965. *Beakers from Northumberland*. Newcastle Upon Tyne: Oriel Press.

Tolan-Smith, C. 1997. The Stone Age Landscape: the Contribution of Fieldwalking. In C. Tolan-Smith (ed.) *Landscape Archaeology in Tynedale*. Newcastle upon Tyne: University of Newcastle upon Tyne: 79-89.

Topping, P. 2003. Grime's Graves. London: English Heritage Guidebook.

Trechmann, C.T. 1936. Mesolithic Flints from the Submerged Forest at West Hartlepool. *Proceedings of the Prehistoric Society* 2: 161-8.

Tyldesley, J.A. 1987. *The Bout Coupé Handaxe. A Typological Problem*. Oxford: Britsh Archaeological Reports, British Series 170.

Van Peer, P. 1992. *The Levallois Reduction Strategy*. Madison: Prehistory Press (Monographs in World Archaeology No. 13).

Vang Peterson, P. 1984. Chronological and regional variation in the Late Mesolithic of Eastern Denmark. *Journal of Danish Archaeology* 3: 7-18.

Vang Peterson, P. 1993. *Fra Danmarks Oldtid*. Copenhagen: Høst and Søn.

Verhart, L.B.M. 1995. Fishing for the Mesolithic. The North Sea: A Submerged Mesolithic Landscape. In A. Fischer. (ed.) *Man and Sea in the Mesolithic: Coastal Settlement Above and Below Present Sea Level*. Proceedings of the International Symposium, Kalundborg, Denmark 1993. Oxford: Oxbow Books: 291-302.

Waddington, C. 1998. Cup and ring marks in context. *Cambridge Archaeological Journal* 8(1): 29-54.

Waddington, C. 1999a. *A Landscape Archaeological Study of the Mesolithic-Neolithic in the Milfield Basin, Northumberland*. Oxford: British Archaeological Reports, British Series 291.

Waddington, C. 1999b. Recent lithic finds from Bowden Doors. *Archaeologia Aeliana* 5th ser. 27: 173-4.

Waddington, C. 2000. Recent research on the Mesolithic in the Milfield Basin, Northumberland. In R. Young (ed.) *Mesolithic Lifeways: Current Research in Britain and Ireland*. Leicester: Leicester Archaeology Monograph 5: 165-77.

Waddington, C. 2001a. The Lithic Assemblage. In N. Hodgson, G.C. Stobbs and M. van der Veen. An Iron Age settlement and remains of earlier prehistoric date beneath South Shields Roman Fort, Tyne and Wear. *Archaeological Journal* 158: 62-160.

Waddington, C. 2001b. *Maelmin. An Archaeological Guide*. Milfield, Wooler: CS Publishing.

Waddington, C., Blood, K. and Crow, J.G. 1998. Survey and excavation at Harehaugh Hillfort and possible Neolithic enclosure. *Northern Archaeology* 15/16: 87-108

Waddington, C. and Davies, J. 2002. An Early Neolithic Settlement and Late Bronze Age Burial Cairn near Bolam Lake, Northumberland: fieldwalking, excavation and reconstruction. *Archaeologia Aeliana* 5th Ser. 30: 1-47.

Waddington, C. and Schofield, D. 1999. A new stone-axe source in the Cheviot Hills, Northumberland. *Archaeologia Aeliana* 5th Ser. 27: 175-6.

Waddington, C., Bailey, G., Bayliss, A., Boomer, I., Milner, M., Pedersen, K. and Shiel, R. 2003. A Mesolithic settlement site at Howick, Northumberland: a preliminary report. *Archaeologia Aeliana* 5th ser 32: 1-12

Wainwright, G.J. 1979. *Mount Pleasant, Dorset: Excavations 1970-1971 Incorporating an Account of Excavations undertaken at Woodhenge in 1970*. London: Reports of the Research Committee of the Society of Antiquaries of London No. 37.

Wainwright, G.J. and Longworth, I.H. 1971. *Durrington Walls: Excavations 1966-1968*. London: Reports of the Research Committee of the Society of Antiquaries of London No. 29.

Watson, W. 1968. *Flint Implements. An Account of Stone Age Techniques and Cultures.* London: British Museum.

Weyman, J. 1975. Mesolithic occupation at Gallowhill Farm, Corbridge. *Archaeologia Aeliana* 5th Ser. 3: 219-20.

Weyman, J. 1980. A flint chipping site at Low Shilford, Riding Mill, Northumberland. *Archaeologia Aeliana* 5th Ser. 8: 159-61.

Weyman, J. 1984. The Mesolithic in North-East England. In R. Miket and C. Burgess (eds.) *Between And Beyond The Walls: Essays in Honour of George Jobey.* Edinburgh: John Donald: 38-51.

Whittaker, J.C. 1994. *Flintknapping. Making and Understanding Stone Tools.* Austin: University of Texas Press.

Whittle, A. 1996. *Europe in the Neolithic. The Creation of New Worlds.* Cambridge: Cambridge University Press.

Wickham-Jones, C.R. 1990. *Rhum. Mesolithic and Later Sites at Kinloch. Excavations 1984-86.* Edinburgh: Society of Antiquaries of Scotland.

Wickham-Jones, C.R. and Collins, G.H. 1978. The sources of flint and chert in northern Britain. *Proceedings of the Society of Antiquaries of Scotland* 109: 7-19.

Wickham-Jones, C.R. and Dalland, M. 1998. A small Mesolithic site at Fife Ness, Scotland. *Internet Archaeology* Issue 5: 6.3.

Williams, L.A. and Crerar, D.A. 1985. Silica Diagenesis, II: General Mechanisms. *Journal of Sedimentary Petrology* 55: 312-21.

Wright, R.V.S. (ed.) 1977. *Stone Tools as Cultural Markers.* Canberra: Australian Institute of Aboriginal Studies.

Wymer, J. 1962. Excavations at the Maglemosian sites at Thatcham, Berkshire, England. *Proceedings of the Prehistoric Society* 28: 329-61.

Wymer, J. 1968. Lower *Palaeolithic Archaeology in Britain as Represented by the Thames Valley.* London: John Baker Ltd.

Wymer, J. 1982. *The Palaeolithic Age.* London: Croom Helm.

Wymer, J. 1991. *Mesolithic Britain.* Princes Risborough: Shire.

Wymer, J. 1999. *The Lower Palaeolithic Occupation of Britain.* (Volumes 1 and 2). Salisbury: Wessex Archaeology and English Heritage.

Young, R. 1980. Prehistoric Weardale. In *The Archaeology of the Durham Dales.* Report of the Durham Archaeological Committee on the archaeology of the area covered by Durham County Council's 'Durham Dales Plan', 5-8 and 37-40.

Young, R. 1984. Potential Sources of Flint and Chert in the North-East of England. *Lithics* 5: 3-9.

Young, R. 1987. *Lithics and Subsistence in North-Eastern England. Aspects of the Prehistoric Archaeology of the Wear Valley, County Durham from the Mesolithic to the Bronze Age.* Oxford: British Archaeological reports, Britsh Series 161.

Young, R. 1989. Mixed lithic scatters and the Mesolithic-Neolithic transition in the north-east of England: a speculation. In I. Brooks and P. Phillips (eds.) *Breaking the Stony Silence. Papers from the Sheffield Lithics Conference 1988.* Oxford: British Archaeological Reports, British Series 213: 161-185.

Young, R. 2000. Aspects of the 'coastal Mesolithic' of the north east of England. In R. Young (ed.) *Mesolithic Lifeways. Current Research from Britain and Ireland.* Leicester: University of Leicester Archaeology Monographs No. 7: 179-190.

Young, R., Coggins, D. and Laurie, T. 1989. The late Upper Palaeolithic and Mesolithic of the North Pennine Dales in the light of recent research. In C. Bonsall (ed.) *The Mesolithic in Europe: Proceedings of the 3rd International Mesolithic Symposium, Edinburgh,* 164-174.

Young, R. and Humphrey, J. 1999. Flint use in England after the Bronze Age: time for a re-evaluation? *Proceedings of the Prehistoric Society* 65: 231-242.

Index